COMMUNICATION SKILLS FOR BEGINNERS

Learn To Talk To Anybody, Crush Social Anxiety,

Boost Public Speaking, Have Fun, Be A Winner

RICHARD DAVIDS

This book is dedicated to all those who aspire to unlock the doors of effective communication. To the individuals who believe in the power of words, the art of connection, and the possibility of growth through understanding.

May these pages serve as a source of inspiration and guidance on your journey to communication mastery. Whether you're a seasoned communicator or just beginning to explore the depths of human connection, this book is for you.

In the spirit of learning, growth, and the boundless potential of effective communication, I dedicate this work to you.

TABLE OF CONTENTS

Introduction

In a world brimming with endless possibilities, effective communication is the bridge that connects us to our aspirations, our dreams, and the people who surround us. Have you ever found yourself wishing you could engage in a captivating conversation, conquer your social anxiety, or speak with the confidence of a winner? If so, then "Communication Skills for Beginners" is your ticket to transforming those desires into reality.

In the pages of this book, we will embark on a remarkable journey together, where you'll unlock the secrets to becoming a confident communicator. With the guidance of Richard Davids, an expert in the field, you'll gain the knowledge and skills needed to talk to anybody, crush social anxiety, boost your public speaking prowess, and infuse your interactions with a sense of fun and accomplishment.

Communication is not merely a tool for conveying words; it's the art of connecting with others, expressing your ideas, and leaving a lasting impression. As we dive into the principles, techniques, and strategies within these pages, you'll discover that the power of effective communication is within your grasp.

Are you ready to take your first step towards a brighter, more communicative future? If so, let's begin this transformative journey, where you'll learn how to communicate with confidence, overcome your fears, and embrace the joy of being a winner in every interaction.

Why Effective Communication Matters

In the grand tapestry of human experience, communication stands as the golden thread that weaves our connections, shapes our destinies, and paints the vivid canvas of our lives. It is the master key that unlocks doors to opportunity, influence, and understanding.

Effective communication isn't just a valuable skill; it's the lifeblood of success, both personally and professionally.

Imagine the power of delivering your thoughts with such clarity that they resonate with your audience, leaving a lasting impact. Envision the confidence to conquer social anxieties and build relationships effortlessly. Visualize the thrill of standing before a crowd, captivating their attention with every word you speak.

Throughout history, great leaders, innovators, and visionaries have harnessed the art of communication to inspire change and elevate humanity. Now, the torch is passed to you. The pages of this book will reveal the transformative potential of mastering the craft of effective communication. The world is yours to navigate, and the journey begins here. As you delve into the secrets of communication, you will uncover the path to becoming a true master of your own destiny.

Your Journey to Communication Mastery

Prepare to embark on a transformative odyssey into the realm of communication mastery. This section is your compass, guiding you through the enchanting landscapes of effective communication. As you set forth on this voyage, you will unravel the techniques, strategies, and insights that will shape you into a confident communicator.

Think of this journey as the golden opportunity to discover not only the power of words but also the art of wielding them with precision. Each chapter will be a stepping stone towards enhancing your communication skills, bolstering your self-assurance, and igniting your passion for this remarkable adventure.

Your destination is the realm of skilled communication, where you'll engage with people effortlessly, conquer public speaking fears, and experience the exhilaration of being a true conversational champion. Brace yourself, for this journey promises not only to be enlightening but also an exciting exploration of your untapped potential. Your odyssey to communication mastery begins now.

PART I: Foundation of Effective Communication

Chapter One: The Art of Listening

Active Listening: The Cornerstone of Communication

In the whirlwind of daily life, amidst the cacophony of voices and the constant hum of digital interactions, we often forget the profound significance of one critical component in effective communication – active listening. This section is dedicated to unraveling the art and science of active listening, a cornerstone of communication mastery. By the time you reach the end, you will not only understand the transformative potential of this skill but also possess the tools to integrate it into your everyday interactions.

The Lost Art of Listening

In a world where everyone seems to be in a hurry to express themselves, genuine listening often takes a back seat. We hear, but do we truly listen? Active listening goes beyond the mere act of hearing; it's a deliberate and focused effort to understand and connect with the speaker. By embracing this art, you open the door to more profound conversations, deeper relationships, and a richer understanding of the world around you.

The Pillars of Active Listening

1. **Engagement**: The foundation of active listening lies in your commitment to the conversation. Engage with the speaker through eye contact, body language, and verbal cues. Show them that you're fully present and ready to absorb their words.

2. **Empathy**: Active listening isn't just about hearing the words but also understanding the emotions and perspectives behind them. Empathy allows you to connect on a deeper level,

showing the speaker that their feelings are acknowledged and respected.

3. **Questioning**: Skillful questioning allows you to dig deeper into the conversation. Open-ended questions encourage the speaker to share more, revealing valuable insights and fostering a sense of trust.

4. **Reflective Responses**: Responding with empathy and understanding demonstrates that you've not only heard the speaker but also internalized their message. Reflective responses validate their feelings and create a safe space for dialogue.

The Art of Silence

In the rush to respond, we often overlook the power of silence. Active listening includes moments of silence, where you allow the speaker to collect their thoughts and continue at their own pace. This pause can be a powerful tool in ensuring that you don't overshadow the speaker's message with your own words.

Overcoming Listening Barriers

Effective active listening requires transcending common barriers that hinder understanding. These barriers include distractions, preconceived notions, and personal biases. By recognizing and addressing these obstacles, you can become a more adept listener and foster more meaningful connections.

Building Rapport Through Listening

One of the most significant benefits of active listening is its ability to build rapport. When you listen with sincerity, you create an environment where others feel valued and respected. This, in turn, enhances your relationships, both personally and professionally, and opens doors to more opportunities.

Practical Exercises and Applications

To truly master active listening, you need to put theory into practice. This section offers practical exercises and real-world applications that allow you to hone your listening skills in everyday situations. From workplace meetings to personal conversations, you'll find guidance on how to apply active listening techniques effectively.

Active listening is not just a skill; it's a mindset, a way of being. As you complete this section, you'll not only appreciate the significance of active listening but also possess the tools to become a more adept communicator. Your journey to communication mastery has begun, and active listening is the compass guiding you toward more profound connections and meaningful dialogues.

Strategies for Improving Your Listening Skills

While understanding the importance of active listening is essential, mastering the art requires a set of concrete strategies and techniques. In this subsection, we will delve into practical methods to enhance your listening skills and become a more effective communicator. These strategies are designed to help you overcome common obstacles and establish a strong foundation for active listening.

1. Remove Distractions

In our fast-paced world, distractions abound. Smartphones, email notifications, and external noises can easily divert your attention from the speaker. The first step in improving your listening skills is to identify and eliminate these distractions. Find a quiet and focused environment where you can engage fully with the conversation.

2. Maintain Eye Contact

Maintaining eye contact with the speaker is a fundamental element of active listening. It signals your attentiveness and interest in what they are saying. While it's not necessary to engage in constant eye contact, especially in culturally diverse contexts, ensuring that you connect visually with the speaker reinforces your commitment to the conversation.

3. Practice Mindfulness

Mindfulness is the practice of being fully present in the moment, which is an invaluable skill for active listening. Clear your mind of preoccupations, judgments, and distractions. Focus your attention entirely on the speaker and their message. Mindfulness allows you to absorb the information more effectively and respond with empathy.

4. Avoid Interrupting

Interruptions can disrupt the flow of the conversation and indicate impatience. Give the speaker space to share their message and be prepared to respond after they have completed their point.

5. Paraphrase and Reflect

A powerful technique in active listening is paraphrasing and reflecting the speaker's words. After they've spoken, rephrase their message in your own words to confirm your understanding. This not only demonstrates that you're actively listening but also allows for immediate clarification if needed.

6. Show Empathy

Empathy is a cornerstone of active listening. Acknowledge their feelings and demonstrate compassion. This not only fosters a deeper connection but also encourages the speaker to share more openly.

7. Ask Clarifying Questions

When you encounter ambiguous or unclear information, don't hesitate to ask clarifying questions. These questions can help you gain a more comprehensive understanding of the speaker's message and show that you're genuinely engaged in the conversation.

8. Practice Patience

Active listening requires patience. Sometimes, the speaker may need time to collect their thoughts or express themselves fully. Avoid rushing the conversation and give the speaker the time they need to communicate effectively.

By incorporating these strategies into your listening skills, you'll not only enhance your ability to absorb information but also create a conducive atmosphere for more meaningful and productive conversations. As you continue to refine these techniques, you'll find that your communication with others becomes more impactful and satisfying.

Chapter Two: The Power of Words

Crafting Impactful Messages

Communication is a two-way street, and while active listening is crucial, equally significant is your ability to convey your thoughts and ideas effectively. This subsection is dedicated to unraveling the art of crafting impactful messages that resonate with your audience, leaving a lasting impression and facilitating clearer communication. We will explore the elements that make a message powerful and the techniques to enhance your message creation skills.

The Power of Clarity

Clarity is the cornerstone of impactful communication. A clear message ensures that your audience understands your intention and the information you're conveying. To craft a message with clarity:

- Define your purpose: Understand the goal of your message and what you want to achieve.

- Organize your thoughts: Structure your message logically to ensure that your points flow smoothly.

- Use plain language: Avoid jargon and complex terms, making your message accessible to a broad audience.

The Impact of Conciseness

A concise message not only holds the listener's attention but also ensures that your main points are easily digestible. To create concise messages:

- Trim unnecessary information: Remove any superfluous details that do not contribute to the message's core purpose.

- Use bullet points or lists: When appropriate, breaking down information into lists or bullet points can enhance comprehension.

Harnessing the Power of Storytelling

One of the most potent methods of message crafting is storytelling. Stories have the unique ability to captivate, engage, and create a memorable impact. To incorporate storytelling into your messages:

- Use personal anecdotes: Share relevant personal experiences that connect with the message's theme.

- Create a narrative arc: Structure your message like a story, with a beginning, middle, and end.

The Art of Persuasion

Crafting impactful messages often involves persuasion, especially when you're trying to influence or convince your audience. To make your messages more persuasive:

- Understand your audience: Tailor your message to your audience's needs, interests, and concerns.

- Use persuasive techniques: Employ rhetorical devices, such as ethos, pathos, and logos, to appeal to your audience's emotions, ethics, and logic.

The Role of Visual Aids

In some situations, visual aids can enhance your message significantly. They provide a visual representation of your content, making complex ideas more accessible. To utilize visual aids effectively:

- Choose the right medium: Select visuals that are appropriate for your message, such as charts, graphs, or images.

- Keep it simple: Ensure that your visual aids are not overly cluttered and reinforce your message.

Crafting impactful messages is an essential skill for anyone seeking to communicate effectively. By focusing on clarity, conciseness, storytelling, persuasion, and visual aids, you'll be better equipped to create messages that engage your audience and leave a lasting impact. As you continue to hone these skills, your ability to express your thoughts and ideas clearly and powerfully will become second nature, enriching your communication repertoire.

Choosing the Right Words for Different Audiences

Effective communication goes beyond the message itself; it encompasses the art of tailoring your words to suit your audience's needs, expectations, and preferences. This subsection delves into the strategies and techniques for choosing the right words for different audiences, enabling you to connect on a deeper level and convey your message with greater impact.

Understanding Your Audience

Before you can choose the right words, it's imperative to understand your audience. Consider the following aspects when analyzing your listeners:

- **Demographics**: Age, gender, education level, and cultural background all play a role in how your message is received.

- **Psychographics**: What are the interests, values, and beliefs of your audience? Understanding their psychographics can help you frame your message appropriately.

- **Context**: The context in which your message is delivered matters. Is it a formal presentation, a casual conversation, or an academic setting?

Tailoring Your Language

Once you've gained insight into your audience, it's time to tailor your language to their preferences. Here's how to do it effectively:

- **Simplify or Elevate**: Depending on your audience's level of expertise, you may need to simplify or elevate your language. Avoid jargon with non-expert audiences, but use specialized terminology when communicating with experts.

- **Tone and Style**: Adjust your tone and style to match your audience's expectations. For a professional setting, maintain a formal tone, but in a casual conversation, a more informal style may be appropriate.

- **Emotional Resonance**: Choose words and phrases that resonate with your audience's emotions. If they value security, use language that emphasizes safety and reliability.

The Power of Analogies and Metaphors

Analogies and metaphors can be incredibly effective in conveying complex ideas to different audiences. These tools help your audience relate to the message by connecting it to something familiar. Be sure to select analogies and metaphors that are relevant to your audience's experiences and interests.

Audience Engagement and Interaction

In some settings, involving your audience can enhance the message's reception. Encourage questions, discussions, or feedback. This interaction not only gauges your audience's understanding but also allows for real-time adjustments in your language and content.

Adapting in Real-Time

The ability to adapt in real-time is a valuable skill in choosing the right words for different audiences. Pay attention to your audience's reactions and adjust your language and approach as necessary. Being flexible and responsive is key to ensuring effective communication.

Choosing the right words for different audiences is a dynamic and responsive process. By understanding your audience's demographics, psychographics, and context, you can tailor your language effectively. Incorporating analogies and metaphors, encouraging audience engagement, and adapting in real-time will further refine your communication skills. As you continue to practice and refine these techniques, you'll become a more adept communicator, capable of connecting with a wide range of audiences and conveying your message with precision and resonance.

Chapter Three: Non-Verbal Communication

Understanding Body Language

In the intricate realm of human communication, words are just one part of the equation. Our bodies, in their infinite subtlety, speak volumes. Body language is a universal dialect, understood across cultures and languages. It's the unspoken conversation that complements and often overrides our verbal expressions. This subsection delves into the world of body language, its intricacies, and the profound impact it can have on our interactions.

The Silent Symphony of Non-Verbal Cues

Before we dive into the nuances of body language, let's take a moment to appreciate the symphony of non-verbal cues that make up this silent language:

- **Gestures**: Our hands, arms, and facial expressions convey a multitude of emotions and intentions.

- **Posture**: The way we hold ourselves, whether we stand tall or slouch, communicates confidence, attentiveness, or indifference.

- **Eye Contact**: The windows to our soul, our eyes reveal our emotions, interests, and sincerity.

- **Microexpressions**: Fleeting, involuntary facial expressions that reveal our true feelings before we can mask them with a more controlled expression.

- **Proxemics**: The use of space in communication, including how close or far we stand from others.

Understanding these elements of body language equips us to decode the unspoken messages in our daily interactions. Let's explore how to decipher and utilize this knowledge effectively.

Decoding Non-Verbal Cues

1. Gestures and Expressions

Our gestures and expressions are a treasure trove of insights. They often reveal more about our feelings and intentions than our words ever could. The key is to observe them in context. Here are some fundamental gestures and expressions to consider:

- **Open and Closed Postures**: An open posture, arms relaxed and open, indicates receptiveness, while crossed arms may signal defensiveness or discomfort.

- **Smiles**: Not all smiles are equal. A genuine smile reaches the eyes and involves the entire face, while a forced smile often only involves the mouth.

2. Eye Contact

The eyes are perhaps the most potent tools for non-verbal communication. Proper eye contact can convey engagement, sincerity, and interest. However, the nuances of eye contact vary across cultures. It's crucial to be aware of these variations while maintaining respectful and meaningful eye contact.

3. Microexpressions

Microexpressions are fleeting and often go unnoticed, but they can be a treasure trove of truth. Learning to recognize these subtle expressions can provide profound insights into a person's true emotions. While there are various microexpressions, some common ones include surprise, fear, and disgust.

4. Proxemics

Proxemics, or the use of space, varies between cultures and individuals. Understanding these differences is vital. Some may prefer close, intimate spaces in conversation, while others may require more distance to feel comfortable. Failing to respect these boundaries can result in discomfort or even conflict.

Enhancing Your Own Body Language

Understanding body language isn't just about decoding others; it's also about using your own non-verbal cues effectively. Here are some ways to enhance your own body language:

- **Maintain Open Postures**: Stand or sit with an open posture to convey openness and confidence.

- **Engage in Active Listening**: Demonstrating that you are genuinely listening, through nods and other cues, can create a more meaningful connection.

- **Mind Your Facial Expressions**: Be mindful of your facial expressions to ensure they align with your words and intentions.

Cultural Considerations

Body language varies significantly from one culture to another. While some cues are universal, the interpretation of others can be culture-specific. It's essential to be aware of these cultural differences when communicating with individuals from diverse backgrounds. Always approach cross-cultural communication with sensitivity and a willingness to learn.

Understanding body language is a formidable tool in your communication arsenal. It empowers you to decipher hidden emotions, intentions, and meanings in the people you interact with. Furthermore, it enables you to fine-tune your own non-verbal cues to convey sincerity, confidence, and empathy. As you delve deeper into this silent language, you'll uncover the mysteries of human interaction and be better equipped to engage with others on a profound level.

Mastering Non-Verbal Cues for Enhanced Communication

In the fascinating world of human interaction, words are just part of the story. We're all part of an intricate dance where our bodies communicate as much as our mouths. Understanding and mastering non-verbal cues can unlock a whole new dimension of effective communication.

The Unspoken Language

Picture this: You're in a meeting, and a colleague's crossed arms and furrowed brow are sending signals that they might not be on board with your idea, even though they haven't said a word. That's the power of non-verbal cues – the messages we send through our body language, gestures, and expressions.

Open Up with Open Postures

Ever notice how you automatically feel more comfortable and open when someone stands or sits with a relaxed, open posture? Open postures signal receptiveness, confidence, and a willingness to engage. It's like a warm welcome without saying a word.

The Eyes Have It

And it's true! Proper eye contact can convey sincerity, interest, and attentiveness. But here's the trick: not all eye contact is created equal. In some cultures, extended eye contact may be seen as assertive, while in others, it could be considered rude. It's crucial to find the balance that suits the context and the people you're communicating with.

The Hidden Truth: Microexpressions

Microexpressions are those fleeting, almost invisible facial expressions that reveal our true feelings, often before we can consciously mask them. They're like emotional truth serum. While there are several microexpressions, the universal ones include surprise, fear, disgust, and more. Recognizing these tiny, potent signals can give you profound insights into someone's emotions.

Respect Personal Space

You've probably noticed that some people prefer standing closer during conversations, while others like a bit more space. This is the concept of proxemics, or the use of space in communication. Respecting personal space is essential to ensure that everyone feels comfortable and respected during the conversation.

Enhance Your Non-Verbal Language

It's not just about understanding non-verbal cues; it's also about using your own body language effectively. To do this, you can:

- Keep an open posture to convey confidence and openness.

- Engage actively in listening through nods and other cues to show your attentiveness.

- Be mindful of your facial expressions to ensure they align with your words and intentions.

Remember the Cultural Context

Non-verbal cues can vary widely across cultures. What's a sign of respect in one culture might be a sign of disrespect in another. Always be aware of these cultural differences and approach cross-cultural communication with sensitivity and curiosity.

In Conclusion

Mastering non-verbal cues is like having a secret decoder for human interaction. It empowers you to understand hidden emotions, intentions, and meanings in the people you interact with. It also enables you to fine-tune your own non-verbal cues to express sincerity, confidence, and empathy. As you delve deeper into this fascinating world, you'll become a more skilled communicator, engaging with others on a profound level that goes beyond words.

PART II: Overcoming Communication Barriers

Chapter Four: Breaking Down Barriers

Identifying Common Obstacles to Effective Communication

Effective communication can sometimes feel like navigating a maze, with obstacles that impede the smooth flow of information and understanding. In this subsection, we will explore the common obstacles to effective communication and equip you with the knowledge and strategies to overcome them. By understanding these roadblocks, you'll be better prepared to communicate with clarity and precision.

Noise and Distractions

Communication can be disrupted by external factors that create noise and distractions. Noisy environments, interruptions, or even digital distractions can hinder the effectiveness of a conversation. Identifying and mitigating these disturbances is crucial to maintaining clear and focused communication.

Assumptions and Stereotypes

We often carry assumptions and stereotypes that color our perceptions of others. Preconceived notions can lead to misunderstandings and misinterpretations. To overcome this obstacle, it's essential to approach communication with an open mind and a willingness to challenge and question your assumptions.

Emotional Barriers

Emotions play a significant role in communication. Fear, anger, or anxiety can distort our messages and lead to conflicts or miscommunications. Recognizing and managing your emotions during conversations is vital for maintaining effective communication.

Language Barriers

Language differences can be a significant obstacle, especially in multicultural or global settings. Misunderstandings can arise from language nuances, idiomatic expressions, and accents. In such cases, it's essential to adapt your communication style to ensure clarity and understanding.

Lack of Clarity

Ineffective communication often results from a lack of clarity in the message. Using vague language, jargon, or excessive complexity can hinder comprehension. To overcome this obstacle, focus on simplicity, precision, and ensuring that your message aligns with the intended audience's level of understanding.

Active Listening Deficits

Communication is a two-way process, and active listening is as crucial as effective speaking. Failing to listen actively, interrupting, or not providing feedback can obstruct the flow of a conversation. To address this, emphasize active listening techniques and create a receptive environment for dialogue.

Misaligned Expectations

Communication breakdowns can occur when individuals have different expectations about the conversation's purpose and outcome. To avoid this obstacle, it's beneficial to establish clear goals and intentions for the conversation and ensure that all parties are on the same page.

Lack of Feedback

Feedback is essential for validating the success of communication. Without feedback, you may not know if your message was understood as intended. Encouraging feedback and asking clarifying questions can help prevent misunderstandings and enhance communication.

Overcoming the Obstacles

Identifying common obstacles to effective communication is the first step toward overcoming them. By recognizing these challenges and implementing strategies to address them, you can enhance your communication skills and minimize the roadblocks that hinder clear and meaningful interactions. The next time you encounter one of these obstacles, you'll be better prepared to navigate through the maze of communication and reach your destination with greater clarity and success.

Techniques to Overcome Communication Roadblocks

In the vast landscape of human communication, roadblocks are a common occurrence. These obstacles can obstruct the free flow of ideas, intentions, and understanding between individuals. But fear not, for in this comprehensive subsection, we'll explore a myriad of techniques to overcome these communication roadblocks. By learning how to navigate these obstacles effectively, you'll become a more skilled communicator and a master of clarity and connection.

Active Listening: The Foundation of Effective Communication

One of the most potent techniques for overcoming communication roadblocks is active listening. Here's how to harness the power of active listening:

1. **Maintain Eye Contact**: Show the speaker that you're fully present and attentive by maintaining eye contact. This simple gesture conveys your interest and receptiveness.

2. **Use Nonverbal Cues**: Nonverbal cues, such as nods, smiles, and facial expressions, signal that you're actively listening and encouraging the speaker to continue sharing their thoughts.

3. **Reflect and Paraphrase**: After the speaker has conveyed their message, reflect on what you've heard and paraphrase it in your words. This not only confirms your understanding but also encourages the speaker to elaborate on their points.

4. **Ask Open-Ended Questions**: Encourage the speaker to delve deeper into their thoughts and feelings by asking open-ended questions. These questions invite more extensive responses and help in uncovering hidden roadblocks.

Breaking Down Emotional Barriers

Emotions can be a significant roadblock in communication, but they can also be an opportunity for connection. Here's how to break down emotional barriers:

1. **Embrace Empathy**: Make an effort to understand the speaker's emotions and feelings. Demonstrating empathy and acknowledging their emotional state can create a safe space for open dialogue.

2. **Manage Your Emotions**: If you find that your emotions are hindering effective communication, take a moment to manage them. A deep breath, a pause, or a change in perspective can help you regain control.

3. **Use "I" Statements**: When discussing sensitive or emotional topics, use "I" statements to express your feelings and perspectives. This approach promotes open conversation without triggering defensive responses.

Clear Language and Clarity

Clear language is the bridge over many communication roadblocks. To ensure clarity:

1. **Simplify Your Message**: Avoid jargon, complex terms, or excessive technical language. Use plain language that is accessible to your audience.

2. **Structure Your Message**: Organize your thoughts logically to ensure that your message flows coherently. A well-structured message is easier to follow and comprehend.

3. **Check for Understanding**: Periodically pause during the conversation to check for the listener's understanding. This ensures that you're on the same page and can address any points of confusion.

Navigating Cultural Differences

In our interconnected world, cultural differences can create significant communication roadblocks.

1. **Cultural Sensitivity**: Approach cross-cultural communication with cultural sensitivity. Make an effort to understand and respect the cultural norms and practices of the people you are communicating with.

2. **Adapt Your Communication**: Be flexible in adapting your communication style to suit the cultural preferences of your audience. This might involve adjusting your tone, gestures, and level of formality.

Feedback and Clarification

Feedback is a powerful tool for overcoming communication roadblocks. It allows both the speaker and the listener to ensure they are on the same page. Here's how to use feedback effectively:

1. **Encourage Feedback**: Create a space for open and honest feedback. Encourage the listener to ask questions, seek clarification, and share their thoughts.

2. **Ask Clarifying Questions**: When you sense confusion or ambiguity, don't hesitate to ask clarifying questions. These questions help pinpoint the roadblocks and pave the way for clear communication.

Identifying Misaligned Expectations

Misaligned expectations can lead to communication roadblocks. To avoid these obstacles:

1. **Set Clear Goals**: Define the purpose and expectations of the conversation at the outset. This ensures that all parties are aligned with the conversation's goals and outcomes.

2. **Clarify Intentions**: During the conversation, periodically revisit the goals and intentions to ensure that everyone remains on the same page.

Respecting Personal Space and Boundaries

Misunderstandings often occur when personal space and boundaries are not respected. To overcome this roadblock:

1. **Be Mindful of Space**: Respect personal space and boundaries, and be aware of cultural variations. Ensure that your physical proximity is comfortable for the listener.

2. **Ask for Consent**: When addressing sensitive or personal topics, ask for consent to broach these subjects. Respecting personal boundaries fosters trust and open communication.

Conclusion

The journey through communication roadblocks is a path of continuous learning and improvement. By implementing these techniques, you'll develop the skills to navigate the complex terrain of human interaction effectively. As you incorporate active listening, emotional awareness, clear language, and cultural sensitivity into your communication toolbox, you'll find that communication roadblocks become mere stepping stones to deeper understanding and connection. With these techniques, you're well on your way to becoming a master of effective communication.

Chapter Five: Conflict Resolution and Difficult Conversations

Navigating Conflicts with Diplomacy

Conflict is a natural part of human interaction. Whether it's in the workplace, within relationships, or in social settings, conflicts can arise due to differing opinions, goals, and values. However, mastering the art of conflict resolution with diplomacy is a valuable skill. In this subsection, we will explore techniques to navigate conflicts with grace and diplomacy, turning potentially turbulent situations into opportunities for growth and understanding.

Understanding the Nature of Conflict

Before delving into the strategies of conflict resolution, it's essential to understand the nature of conflict. Conflict can manifest in various forms:

- **Interpersonal Conflict**: Disagreements between individuals based on personal differences or misunderstandings.

- **Intrapersonal Conflict**: An internal struggle within an individual, such as conflicting emotions or values.

- **Group Conflict**: Conflict that arises within a group, team, or organization, often stemming from differing goals or priorities.

Understanding the underlying causes of conflict can guide your approach to resolution. It's crucial to recognize that conflicts are not inherently negative; they can lead to growth and improved relationships if handled effectively.

The Diplomacy of Active Listening

Active listening, as discussed in previous sections, plays a vital role in conflict resolution. To navigate conflicts with diplomacy, apply active listening techniques:

1. **Create a Safe Space**: Ensure that both parties feel safe and respected during the conversation.

2. **Listen Actively**: Engage in attentive listening to understand the perspectives and emotions of both sides.

3. **Acknowledge Emotions**: Recognize the emotions involved and express empathy. Acknowledging feelings can help defuse tension.

Open Communication

Fostering open and honest communication is the cornerstone of conflict resolution with diplomacy. Here's how to promote open communication:

1. **Set the Stage**: Create a conducive environment for dialogue, free from interruptions and distractions.

2. **Use "I" Statements**: Encourage both parties to express their thoughts and feelings using "I" statements to convey their perspectives without blame.

3. **Ask Open-Ended Questions**: Promote a deeper understanding by asking open-ended questions that encourage elaboration and reflection.

Finding Common Ground

To navigate conflicts with diplomacy, it's essential to seek common ground and shared objectives:

1. **Identify Common Goals**: Discover shared objectives and values that can serve as a foundation for resolution.

2. **Highlight Mutual Benefits**: Emphasize the benefits of reaching a resolution for both parties, demonstrating that cooperation is in their best interest.

Dealing with Emotions

Emotions often run high during conflicts. Diplomacy involves addressing emotions constructively:

1. **Emotional Regulation**: Encourage individuals to manage their emotions and express them in a healthy way.

2. **Empathy**: Promote empathy by helping both parties understand each other's emotional experiences.

3. **Avoid Escalation**: Prevent the escalation of emotional conflicts by staying calm and composed.

Seeking Win-Win Solutions

In many conflicts, seeking a win-win solution is the ideal outcome. Diplomacy involves finding solutions that benefit both parties:

1. **Brainstorming**: Encourage creative problem-solving by brainstorming potential solutions that address the interests of all parties.

2. **Compromise**: Finding middle ground or making concessions can lead to mutually satisfying agreements.

3. **Conflict Transformation**: In some cases, conflict resolution may require a transformation of the conflict into an opportunity for growth and positive change.

Cultural Considerations

Cross-cultural conflicts can present unique challenges. Diplomacy in such situations involves understanding and respecting cultural differences:

1. **Cultural Sensitivity**: Recognize and respect cultural norms, values, and communication styles.

2. **Avoid Assumptions**: Avoid making assumptions based on your own cultural perspective and be open to learning about other cultures.

Escalation and De-escalation

In conflict resolution, it's essential to be aware of escalation and de-escalation techniques:

1. **Early Intervention**: Address conflicts as early as possible to prevent them from escalating.

2. **De-escalation Strategies**: When conflicts intensify, employ de-escalation techniques, such as active listening, compromise, or seeking a time-out to cool off.

Mediation and Third-Party Involvement

In situations where conflicts are particularly complex or intractable, mediation by a neutral third party can be beneficial. Diplomacy often involves seeking mediation when direct resolution proves challenging.

Navigating conflicts with diplomacy is a skill that can transform challenges into opportunities for growth, understanding, and stronger relationships. By understanding the nature of conflict, practicing active listening, fostering open communication, finding common ground, addressing emotions constructively, and seeking win-win solutions, you can become a proficient diplomat in the realm of conflict resolution. Whether in personal relationships, the workplace, or within groups, the ability to navigate conflicts with grace and diplomacy is a valuable asset that can lead to more harmonious interactions and positive outcomes.

Strategies for Handling Tough Discussions

Tough discussions are an inevitable part of life. Whether you need to address a sensitive topic with a loved one, negotiate a challenging situation at work, or navigate a potentially conflict-ridden conversation, having a toolkit of strategies for handling tough discussions is invaluable. In this comprehensive subsection, we'll explore a wide range of techniques and approaches to help you navigate these conversations with confidence and finesse.

Preparing for Tough Discussions

The journey to a successful tough discussion often begins with careful preparation. Here's how to get started:

1. **Clarify Your Objectives**: Define your goals and what you hope to achieve through the discussion. Having clear objectives will guide your approach.

2. **Gather Information**: Ensure you have all the relevant information and facts at your disposal. Being well-informed empowers you to make your points effectively.

3. **Choose the Right Time and Place**: Timing and location can significantly impact the success of your discussion. Select a time when both parties can focus, and a private, quiet setting where you won't be interrupted.

4. **Anticipate Reactions**: Consider how the other party might react and prepare for potential responses and emotions. This foresight will help you stay composed.

Effective Communication Strategies

Effective communication is at the heart of handling tough discussions. These strategies can enhance your communication skills:

1. **Active Listening**: As previously discussed, active listening involves fully engaging with the speaker. Practice this technique to ensure you understand and address the other party's concerns.

2. **Use "I" Statements**: Express your feelings, thoughts, and concerns using "I" statements.

3. **Empathetic Communication**: Show empathy by acknowledging the other person's emotions and perspective.

4. **Stay Calm**: Emotions can run high in tough discussions, but maintaining your composure is crucial. Take deep breaths, use grounding techniques, or take a short break if necessary.

5. **Ensure that your nonverbal cues align with your message.**

The Art of Asking Questions

Asking the right questions can guide the discussion and uncover important information. Here's how to use this art effectively:

1. **Open-Ended Questions**: Encourage detailed responses by asking open-ended questions. These questions can help the other party express themselves more fully.

2. **Clarifying Questions**: When something is unclear, ask clarifying questions to gain a deeper understanding of the other person's perspective.

3. **Reflective Questions**: Encourage introspection and self-reflection by asking reflective questions. These questions can be particularly useful in personal discussions.

Conflict Resolution Techniques

When tough discussions involve conflict, employing conflict resolution techniques can be helpful:

1. **Mediation**: Consider involving a neutral third party to mediate the discussion, especially if tensions are high and progress is stalling.

2. **Win-Win Solutions**: Strive to find solutions that benefit both parties. This approach promotes collaboration and a sense of shared success.

3. **Compromise**: Be willing to make concessions or find middle ground when it serves the overall objective of the discussion.

4. **Conflict Transformation**: In some cases, the conflict can be transformed into an opportunity for personal or professional growth. Consider whether the discussion can lead to positive change.

Handling Tough Personal Discussions

Personal discussions, such as those with loved ones or friends, often require a unique set of strategies:

1. **Create a Safe Space**: Ensure that the discussion takes place in a comfortable and private environment. Both parties should feel safe to express themselves honestly.

2. **Express Your Emotions**: Don't shy away from expressing your emotions and being vulnerable. This can foster a deeper connection and understanding.

3. **Active Empathy**: Demonstrate empathy by actively acknowledging and validating the other person's feelings. This can strengthen the emotional bond.

Handling Tough Professional Discussions

Professional discussions, such as those at work, require a different set of considerations:

1. **Maintain Professionalism**: Keep the discussion professional and focused on the topic at hand. Avoid personal attacks or emotional outbursts.

2. **Use Constructive Feedback**: Offer feedback that is constructive and solution-oriented. This approach helps identify areas for improvement without creating conflict.

3. **Follow Up**: After the discussion, follow up with clear action items and next steps to ensure that progress is made.

Dealing with Tough Conversations in Groups

In group discussions, managing multiple perspectives and dynamics can be challenging. Here are some strategies for handling tough conversations in group settings:

1. **Facilitation**: Appoint a neutral facilitator to guide the discussion and ensure that everyone has an opportunity to speak.

2. **Ground Rules**: Establish ground rules for the discussion, such as listening without interruption, maintaining respect, and focusing on the issue at hand.

3. **Summary Statements**: Periodically summarize the main points and concerns raised in the discussion to keep everyone on the same page.

Conclusion

Tough discussions are opportunities for growth, understanding, and resolution. By preparing thoroughly, employing effective communication strategies, asking the right questions, and using conflict resolution techniques, you can navigate these conversations with confidence and diplomacy. Whether the discussions are personal or professional, involve one person or a group, or revolve around sensitive or complex topics, the strategies outlined here will equip you to handle tough discussions with finesse and achieve positive outcomes.

PART III: Advanced Communication Skills

Chapter 6: Persuasion and Influence

The Art of Persuasion

Persuasion is a potent tool in communication, a skill that can influence opinions, decisions, and actions. Whether you're looking to convince a colleague, sway a potential client, or inspire change in your personal life, mastering the art of persuasion is a valuable asset. In this subsection, we will delve into the strategies and techniques that can help you become a persuasive communicator, capable of achieving your desired outcomes.

The Psychology of Persuasion

Before we explore specific techniques, it's essential to understand the psychological principles that underlie persuasion. Persuasion operates on several key factors:

1. **Credibility**: People are more likely to be persuaded by those they perceive as credible and knowledgeable. Establishing credibility is a fundamental aspect of persuasive communication.

2. **Emotion**: Emotions play a significant role in persuasion. Appeals to emotion can be highly effective in influencing decisions and actions.

3. **Reciprocity**: The principle of reciprocity suggests that when you give something, people often feel obligated to give something in return. This can be leveraged to persuade others.

4. **Social Proof**: People tend to follow the actions of others, especially if those actions are perceived as popular or correct. Demonstrating social proof can enhance your persuasive efforts.

5. **Consistency**: Humans have a natural inclination to act consistently with their previous commitments and beliefs. Persuasion often involves aligning your message with an individual's existing values and commitments.

Building Trust and Credibility

Credibility is the foundation of persuasion. Without it, your attempts to persuade will likely fall flat.

1. **Establish Expertise**: Demonstrating your expertise in the subject matter can enhance your credibility. Share your knowledge and experience in a relevant, non-boastful way.

2. **Be Transparent**: Honesty and transparency are vital. Concealing information or being deceptive can quickly erode trust.

3. **Use Reliable Sources**: Cite credible sources and references to support your arguments. This reinforces the validity of your message.

4. **Engage in Active Listening**: Show that you value the other person's perspective by actively listening and demonstrating empathy. This builds trust and respect.

Appeals to Emotion

Emotions have a profound impact on decision-making. Utilizing emotional appeals can make your message more persuasive:

1. **Storytelling**: Share personal stories or anecdotes that evoke emotions related to your message. Stories create a connection and resonate on an emotional level.

2. **Use Positive Emotions**: Encourage positive emotions, such as joy, hope, or inspiration, to connect with your audience. Positive emotions are powerful motivators.

3. **Address Negative Emotions**: If your message involves addressing negative emotions, such as fear or concern, offer solutions or a path to alleviating those emotions. The principle of reciprocity suggests that when you provide something valuable, people are inclined to reciprocate. Here's how to leverage this principle in persuasion:

1. **Offer Value**: Provide value to the other person, whether it's through information, assistance, or a small favor. This creates a sense of obligation to reciprocate.

2. **Ask for Feedback**: Seeking feedback or input from the other person can also invoke the principle of reciprocity. When they contribute, they become more receptive to your persuasive message.

Harnessing Social Proof

Social proof is the phenomenon where people follow the actions of others. You can use this to your advantage in persuasion:

1. **Highlight Success Stories**: Share success stories or examples of others who have benefited from the desired action or decision. This demonstrates that others are already on board.

2. **Show Popular Support**: Highlight statistics or evidence of widespread support for your message. Knowing that many others have embraced your idea can sway opinions.

Consistency and Commitment

Encouraging consistency with previous commitments or beliefs can be persuasive:

1. **Alignment with Values**: Frame your message in a way that aligns with the individual's existing values and beliefs. This consistency can make your message more persuasive.

2. **Highlight Past Agreements**: Remind the other person of any past agreements or commitments they've made that are related to your persuasive message.

Counterarguments and Rebuttal

It's essential to anticipate and address counterarguments when striving to persuade. Here's how to handle opposition:

1. **Acknowledge Counterarguments**: Recognize opposing viewpoints and concerns. Ignoring them can undermine your credibility.

2. **Rebuttal with Evidence**: Present counterarguments with factual evidence and logic to demonstrate why your perspective is stronger.

3. **Use Positive Language**: Keep the tone of the discussion positive, even when addressing counterarguments. Negative or confrontational language can hinder persuasion.

The art of persuasion is a nuanced and multifaceted skill that can have a significant impact on your personal and professional life. By understanding the psychological principles at play, building trust and credibility, using emotional appeals, invoking reciprocity, harnessing social proof, and promoting consistency and commitment, you can become a more persuasive communicator. Whether you seek to influence decisions, gain support, or inspire change, the strategies outlined here will empower you to navigate the realm of persuasion with confidence and effectiveness.

Techniques for Gaining Influence and Building Trust

In the realm of effective communication, gaining influence and building trust are foundational elements. The ability to inspire confidence and influence decisions or actions is a valuable skill that can significantly impact your personal and professional relationships. In this comprehensive subsection, we will explore a variety of techniques and strategies to help you establish trust and enhance your influence as a communicator.

Establishing Credibility

Credibility is the cornerstone of gaining influence and building trust. Without it, your efforts may lack the impact you desire. Here are techniques to establish and enhance your credibility:

1. **Demonstrate Expertise**: Showcase your knowledge and expertise in relevant areas. Share your experience and qualifications when applicable, but do so modestly and without arrogance.

2. **Provide Value**: Consistently offer valuable information, insights, or assistance to others. By contributing positively, you position yourself as a valuable resource and gain the trust of those you interact with.

3. **Be Consistent**: Consistency in your words and actions is crucial. Align your behavior with your values and promises to build a reputation for reliability.

4. **Seek Feedback and Adapt**: Actively seek feedback from others and be willing to adapt and improve based on their input. This demonstrates a commitment to growth and responsiveness.

Active Listening and Empathy

Active listening and empathy are powerful tools for gaining influence and building trust. These techniques help you connect with others on a deeper level:

1. **Engage in Active Listening**: Practice attentive, non-judgmental listening when interacting with others.

2. **Ask Open-Ended Questions**: Encourage people to express themselves by asking open-ended questions that promote deeper conversations.

3. **Demonstrate Empathy**: Show empathy by acknowledging and validating the emotions and perspectives of others. This creates a sense of understanding and trust.

4. **Reflect and Paraphrase**: After someone has shared their thoughts, reflect on what you've heard and paraphrase it in your own words. This confirms your understanding and shows that you respect their point of view.

Building Relationships

Building strong relationships is essential for gaining influence and trust. Here's how to nurture meaningful connections:

1. **Create a Positive Environment**: Foster a positive and welcoming atmosphere when interacting with others. Positivity is infectious and encourages trust.

2. **Invest Time and Effort**: Allocate time and effort to building relationships. This may involve maintaining regular contact, offering support, and demonstrating a genuine interest in others' well-being.

3. **Be Transparent and Honest**: Honesty and transparency are vital components of trust. Openly communicate your intentions and share your thoughts and feelings honestly.

4. **Celebrate Successes Together**: Acknowledge and celebrate collective achievements. Sharing success reinforces trust and builds a sense of camaraderie.

Ethical and Principled Behavior

To gain influence and build trust, ethical and principled behavior is indispensable. Upholding high ethical standards and principles demonstrates integrity and reliability:

1. **Consistency with Values**: Ensure that your behavior aligns with your core values and principles. People trust those who consistently uphold their beliefs.

2. **Keep Promises**: Only make promises that you can keep, and then fulfill them. Reliability in keeping your word is essential for trust.

3. **Avoid Gossip and Negativity**: Refrain from engaging in gossip or negative conversations about others. Trust is easily eroded by such behaviors.

4. **Address Conflicts and Mistakes Ethically**: When conflicts arise or mistakes are made, approach them ethically and responsibly. Taking ownership and seeking solutions demonstrates integrity.

Influence Techniques

To gain influence effectively, you can employ specific techniques and strategies that motivate others to take action or make decisions in alignment with your goals:

1. **Social Proof**: Use evidence of others who have supported your ideas or taken similar actions to sway opinions. Demonstrating that your perspective is popular or accepted can be persuasive.

2. **Reciprocity**: When you offer something valuable to others, they often feel obliged to reciprocate. Be generous and give freely, and people are more likely to support you in return.

3. **Scarcity**: Create a sense of scarcity or urgency around your ideas or requests. People are more likely to act when they perceive limited opportunities or resources.

4. **Appeal to Emotion**: Employ emotional appeals that resonate with your audience's values and desires. Addressing emotions can motivate action.

Conflict Resolution

Conflict is an inevitable part of human interactions, and handling it effectively is a critical skill for gaining influence and trust. Use these conflict resolution techniques:

1. **Active Listening**: Listen actively to the concerns and perspectives of others involved in the conflict. This demonstrates a willingness to understand and find common ground.

2. **Seek Win-Win Solutions**: Strive to find solutions that benefit all parties involved. Win-win solutions foster cooperation and trust.

3. **Negotiate and Compromise**: Be open to negotiation and compromise. Finding middle ground can lead to resolutions that satisfy everyone's needs.

4. **Mediation**: If conflicts are particularly complex, consider involving a neutral third party as a mediator to guide the resolution process.

Conclusion

Gaining influence and building trust are processes that require time, effort, and intention. By establishing credibility, practicing active listening and empathy, nurturing relationships, maintaining ethical behavior, employing influence techniques, and mastering conflict resolution, you can become a more influential and trustworthy communicator. Whether in personal relationships or professional interactions, these techniques will empower you to navigate the complex landscape of human connection with grace, effectiveness, and a positive impact.

Chapter 7: Public Speaking Excellence

Preparing for Dynamic Presentations

Dynamic presentations are a powerful means of communication that can inform, persuade, and inspire your audience. Whether you're delivering a business proposal, an educational lecture, or a motivational speech, effective presentation preparation is essential to ensure your message resonates with your audience. In this comprehensive subsection, we will explore a range of techniques and strategies to help you prepare for dynamic presentations that captivate, engage, and leave a lasting impact.

Understanding Your Audience

Before diving into the specifics of presentation preparation, it's crucial to understand your audience. Tailoring your presentation to your audience's needs, preferences, and expectations is the first step in creating a dynamic presentation:

1. **Demographics**: Consider the age, gender, background, and interests of your audience. This information will guide your content and tone.

2. **Knowledge Level**: Assess the knowledge level of your audience regarding the topic. Are they beginners, intermediate, or experts? Adjust your content and explanations accordingly.

3. **Goals and Expectations**: Understand what your audience hopes to gain from your presentation. Are they seeking information, inspiration, or specific solutions? Your content should align with their goals and expectations.

4. **Cultural Sensitivity**: Be aware of cultural differences and sensitivities that may influence your audience's perceptions and responses. Ensure that your presentation is respectful and inclusive.

Defining Your Objectives

Clarity of purpose is essential in presentation preparation. Define your objectives to ensure that your message is focused and impactful:

1. **Primary Objective**: Determine the primary goal of your presentation.

2. **Secondary Objectives**: Identify any secondary goals that support your primary objective. These could be additional information, case studies, or examples that enhance your main message.

3. **Desired Outcome**: What do you want your audience to take away from your presentation? Define the key takeaways that you aim to convey.

4. **Action Steps**: If your presentation aims to inspire action, outline the specific steps or calls to action you want your audience to follow.

Structuring Your Presentation

A well-structured presentation is more accessible and engaging for your audience. Consider these structural elements:

1. **Introduction**: Begin with a compelling introduction that captures your audience's attention.

2. **Main Content**: Organize your main content into logical sections or chapters. Use headings and subheadings to guide your audience through the presentation.

3. **Transitions**: Include smooth transitions between sections to maintain a cohesive flow. Use transition phrases or visual cues to signal shifts in topics or ideas.

4. **Visual Aids**: Incorporate visual aids, such as slides or props, to enhance understanding and engagement. Ensure that visuals are relevant and complement your spoken words.

5. **Conclusion**: Summarize the key points of your presentation in the conclusion. Restate your main message and emphasize the takeaways you want your audience to remember.

6. **Q&A Session**: If applicable, plan a question-and-answer session at the end of your presentation to address any audience inquiries.

Crafting Compelling Content

Dynamic presentations are built on compelling content that resonates with your audience. Consider these content creation strategies:

1. **Clarity and Conciseness**: Strive for clear, concise content. Avoid jargon and complexity, and use straightforward language.

2. **Stories and Examples**: Incorporate stories and real-life examples to illustrate key points and engage your audience emotionally.

3. **Statistics and Data**: Use relevant statistics and data to support your claims and make your content more credible.

4. **Visual Appeal**: Create visually appealing slides or materials to complement your spoken content. Use images, infographics, and diagrams to enhance understanding.

5. **Engaging Elements**: Integrate engaging elements, such as interactive exercises, polls, or demonstrations, to maintain audience involvement.

6. **Analogies and Metaphors**: Use analogies and metaphors to simplify complex concepts and make them relatable.

7. **Relatable Language**: Tailor your language to your audience's level of understanding. Avoid jargon that may be unfamiliar to them.

Rehearsal and Delivery

Effective presentation preparation extends to rehearsal and delivery:

1. **Practice**: Rehearse your presentation multiple times to become familiar with the content and flow.

2. **Timing**: Ensure that your presentation fits within the allotted time. Practice pacing to maintain a comfortable speed.

3. **Visual Aid Review**: If you are using visual aids, thoroughly review and test them to avoid technical issues during your presentation.

4. **Nonverbal Communication**: Pay attention to your body language, facial expressions, and tone of voice. Confident and engaging nonverbal communication is as important as your words.

5. **Engagement Strategies**: Plan audience engagement strategies, such as direct questions, discussions, or audience participation, to keep your audience actively involved.

6. **Managing Nervousness**: If you experience nervousness, practice relaxation techniques, deep breathing, or visualization to manage anxiety.

Handling Questions and Interactions

Prepare for potential questions and interactions with your audience:

1. **Anticipate Questions**: Consider the questions your audience might ask and prepare concise, informative responses.

2. **Active Listening**: During the presentation, actively listen to your audience's reactions and questions.

3. **Maintain Control**: Maintain control of the Q&A session by ensuring that questions and comments stay relevant and on-topic.

4. **Handling Challenges**: Be prepared to handle challenging or confrontational questions with grace and professionalism.

Dynamic presentations are a powerful form of communication that can leave a lasting impact on your audience. Effective presentation preparation involves understanding your audience, defining clear objectives, structuring your content, crafting compelling material, rehearsing and delivering with confidence, and handling questions and interactions with poise. Whether your presentations are in a professional, educational, or personal setting, these techniques will help you captivate and engage your audience, leaving them informed, inspired, and eager to take action.

Techniques for Captivating Your Audience

The art of captivating your audience is a fundamental skill for effective communication. Whether you're delivering a presentation, giving a speech, or engaging in a one-on-one conversation, your ability to capture and maintain your audience's attention is crucial. In this extensive subsection, we will explore a variety of techniques and strategies that will help you captivate your audience and leave a lasting impression.

Understanding the Psychology of Captivation

Before we delve into specific techniques, it's essential to understand the psychological factors that influence captivation:

1. **Attention Span**: Recognize that attention spans can vary among individuals. While some people can focus for longer periods, others may need more frequent engagement.

2. **Relevance**: Your content must be relevant and meaningful to your audience. People are more likely to pay attention if they see the value in what you're presenting.

3. **Emotion**: Emotions play a significant role in capturing attention. Content that elicits emotions, whether positive or negative, tends to be more engaging.

4. **Novelty**: Novel or unexpected information can pique interest. Introduce new perspectives, insights, or angles to keep your audience engaged.

5. **Visual and Auditory Stimulation**: The use of visual aids, dynamic visuals, and auditory cues can enhance engagement. These stimuli complement your spoken words.

Building an Engaging Introduction

The introduction is your first opportunity to captivate your audience. Make it count by employing these strategies:

1. **Hook the Audience**: Start with a compelling hook that grabs your audience's attention. This could be a shocking statistic, a thought-provoking question, a powerful quote, or a captivating story.

2. **Relevance**: Immediately establish the relevance of your content to your audience. Explain why they should care about what you're going to say.

3. **Preview**: Provide a brief overview of what your presentation will cover. This gives your audience a roadmap and a reason to stay engaged.

4. **Engage with a Challenge**: Pose a challenge or a problem that your presentation will address. Engaging your audience in solving this challenge can be a powerful motivator.

Storytelling and Narrative Techniques

Storytelling is a captivating tool that can resonate deeply with your audience. Use these narrative techniques to captivate:

1. **Conflict and Resolution**: Craft narratives that involve conflict or challenges, and lead to satisfying resolutions. Audiences are drawn to stories with compelling arcs.

2. **Character Development**: Develop relatable characters or personas in your stories. Your audience should connect with the characters on an emotional level.

3. **Vivid Imagery**: Use descriptive language to create vivid mental images. Help your audience visualize the scenarios and emotions in your stories.

4. **Surprises and Twists**: Include unexpected elements or plot twists that keep your audience engaged and eager to see what happens next.

5. **Emotional Appeal**: Leverage the emotional power of storytelling. Convey emotions and experiences that resonate with your audience's feelings.

Interactive Elements

Engaging your audience actively can significantly enhance captivation:

1. **Ask Questions**: Pose questions to your audience, encouraging them to think, reflect, or respond. Interactive questions create a two-way dialogue.

2. **Discussions and Group Activities**: If appropriate, incorporate group discussions or activities that encourage collaboration and interaction among your audience members.

3. **Audience Participation**: Encourage active participation by involving your audience in demonstrations, surveys, or hands-on experiences related to your content.

4. **Polls and Surveys**: Use real-time polls or surveys to collect audience feedback and opinions. Sharing the results can be captivating and insightful.

5. **Visual Engagement**: Utilize visual aids, props, or multimedia presentations to enhance the visual and auditory aspects of your content. Visual engagement can complement your spoken words.

Varied Delivery Techniques

Diverse delivery techniques keep your audience engaged by offering a range of stimuli:

1. **Change in Tone and Pace**: Vary your tone of voice and pacing to emphasize key points, convey excitement, or create a sense of suspense.

2. **Body Language**: Utilize expressive body language to communicate enthusiasm, confidence, and engagement.

3. **Humor**: Appropriate humor can captivate your audience by adding a lighthearted and relatable dimension to your presentation.

4. **Visuals and Multimedia**: Use compelling visuals, multimedia, and dynamic slides to complement your spoken content. Visual and auditory elements can be captivating.

5. **Live Demonstrations**: Whenever possible, demonstrate concepts or ideas live. Live demonstrations can be highly engaging and create a sense of authenticity.

Encouraging Critical Thinking

Captivation can also come from intellectual stimulation. Encourage critical thinking by:

1. **Provoking Thought**: Pose thought-provoking questions or dilemmas that require your audience to think critically and problem-solve.

2. **Debate and Discussion**: Engage your audience in debates, discussions, or group dialogues that challenge their perspectives and promote reflection.

3. **Case Studies and Examples**: Share real-life case studies and examples that require analysis and interpretation. These practical scenarios captivate through relevance.

4. **Open-Ended Scenarios**: Present open-ended scenarios or open questions that have no single "right" answer. Encourage your audience to explore various possibilities.

The Power of Visual Aids

Well-designed visual aids can be captivating and reinforce your message:

1. **Relevance**: Ensure that your visual aids are directly relevant to your content and enhance understanding. Irrelevant or overly complex visuals can be distracting.

2. **Simplicity**: Keep your visuals simple and uncluttered. Clear, concise visuals are more captivating and effective.

3. **Use of Color**: Utilize color effectively to draw attention to key points, create visual hierarchy, and enhance the overall aesthetic appeal.

4. **Visual Storytelling**: Tell a visual story through your slides or materials. Create a visual narrative that complements your spoken narrative.

5. **Visual Consistency**: Maintain visual consistency throughout your presentation. Consistency in design and layout can enhance captivation.

6. **Incorporate Infographics**: Infographics can be a captivating way to present complex information in a visually engaging format.

Adapting to Audience Feedback

The ability to adapt to your audience's reactions and feedback is crucial for maintaining captivation:

1. **Active Listening**: Continuously gauge your audience's reactions through active listening. Pay attention to verbal and non-verbal cues.

2. **Adapt and Respond**: Be prepared to adapt your content, pacing, or delivery based on the audience's response. Flexibility enhances captivation.

3. **Engage with Questions**: Encourage questions and engagement throughout your presentation. Address audience inquiries promptly.

4. **Embrace Interaction**: Embrace spontaneous interactions or audience contributions that add depth and authenticity to your presentation.

5. **Feedback Loops**: Create feedback loops by periodically checking in with your audience. Ask if they have questions, if the pacing is comfortable, and if they need clarification.

The Art of Closure

A captivating presentation also requires a compelling closure:

1. **Summarize Key Points**: Summarize the main takeaways of your presentation to reinforce the most crucial information.

2. **End with a Quote**: End with a memorable quote that encapsulates your message or leaves your audience with a powerful thought.

3. **Call to Action**: If your presentation involves inspiring action, provide a clear and motivating call to action that encourages your audience to act on what they've learned.

4. **Leave Room for Reflection**: Allow a moment of reflection or contemplation before concluding. This gives your audience time to absorb and process the content.

5. **Express Gratitude**: Thank your audience for their time and attention. Express appreciation for their engagement.

Handling Challenging Situations

In some instances, you may encounter challenging situations that can disrupt captivation:

1. **Technical Issues**: Be prepared for technical glitches and have backup plans in place. Maintain composure and adapt if technical issues arise.

2. **Distracted Audience**: If your audience appears distracted, refocus their attention with a captivating story, a question, or an engaging visual.

3. **Difficult Questions**: Handle difficult or confrontational questions with grace and professionalism. Maintain a respectful and confident demeanor.

4. **Time Constraints**: If you face time constraints, prioritize key content and adapt your delivery to fit within the allotted time.

5. **Audience Disengagement**: If you sense audience disengagement, actively seek their feedback or ask for their input to reignite their interest.

Conclusion

Captivating your audience is a multifaceted skill that draws upon psychology, storytelling, interaction, adaptability, visual aids, and closure. Whether you're delivering presentations, speeches, or engaging in meaningful conversations, the ability to captivate your audience ensures that your message resonates and leaves a lasting impression. These techniques, when applied thoughtfully and creatively, will empower you to connect with your audience on a profound level, making your communication more engaging, impactful, and memorable.

PART Four: Navigating Social and Professional Realms

Chapter 8: Networking and Building Meaningful Relationships

Cultivating Professional and Personal Networks

Networking is a vital aspect of both professional and personal life. Your ability to connect with others, build relationships, and leverage these connections can have a profound impact on your career, personal development, and overall well-being. In this comprehensive subsection, we will explore a variety of techniques and strategies to help you cultivate and nurture your professional and personal networks effectively.

The Importance of Networking

Before delving into specific techniques, it's essential to understand why networking is crucial:

1. **Opportunities**: Networking opens doors to various opportunities, whether they are career-related, educational, or personal. It can lead to job offers, collaborations, mentorships, and more.

2. **Knowledge and Insights**: Your network can provide you with valuable insights, information, and expertise. Networking allows you to tap into the collective knowledge of your connections.

3. **Support System**: Building a network can create a supportive community. In times of personal or professional challenges, your network can provide guidance, encouragement, and assistance.

4. **Personal Growth**: Interacting with diverse individuals through networking can broaden your horizons and help you develop personally.

5. **Social Well-Being**: Networking isn't limited to professional connections; it also encompasses personal relationships. Cultivating your personal network is vital for emotional support, companionship, and well-being.

Professional Networking

Cultivating a robust professional network is essential for career growth and development. Here are techniques for effective professional networking:

1. **Attend Networking Events**: Participate in industry-specific events, conferences, seminars, and workshops.

2. **Online Networking**: Utilize professional networking platforms such as LinkedIn to connect with colleagues, peers, and industry professionals. Regularly update your profile to showcase your skills and achievements.

3. **Join Professional Associations**: Consider becoming a member of professional associations related to your field. These organizations offer networking events, resources, and opportunities for career advancement.

4. **Mentorship**: Seek out mentors or become a mentor yourself. Mentorship relationships provide guidance, support, and opportunities for personal and professional growth.

5. **Volunteer**: Volunteering in your industry or community can help you build connections and give back to the community. It's also an excellent way to develop new skills and experiences.

6. **Networking Groups**: Join networking groups or clubs specific to your industry or interests. These groups often have regular meetings, events, and opportunities for collaboration.

7. **Follow Up**: After meeting new contacts, ensure that you follow up promptly. Send a thank-you email, connect on LinkedIn, or schedule a follow-up meeting to nurture the relationship.

Personal Networking

Cultivating personal networks is equally important for your overall well-being and support system. Here are techniques for effective personal networking:

1. **Social Gatherings**: Attend social gatherings, parties, and events to meet new people and expand your circle of friends. These casual interactions can lead to meaningful friendships.

2. **Shared Interests**: Engage in hobbies or activities that align with your interests.

3. **Family and Friends**: Maintain and strengthen relationships with family and friends. These connections are often your most reliable sources of emotional support and companionship.

4. **Neighbors and Community**: Get to know your neighbors and engage in community activities. Strong community connections can lead to a sense of belonging and mutual support.

5. **Online Communities**: Participate in online communities and social platforms that align with your interests and passions. Engaging in online discussions can lead to meaningful connections.

6. **Events and Gatherings**: Host your own events and gatherings, such as dinners, game nights, or themed parties. Creating opportunities for social interaction can help you build personal connections.

7. **Be a Good Listener**: When engaging with others, be an active and empathetic listener. Showing genuine interest in their lives and concerns fosters strong relationships.

8. **Help and Support**: Offer your assistance and support to others in your personal network. Being there for friends and family during their challenges can strengthen your bonds.

Building and Nurturing Relationships

Whether in your professional or personal network, the process of building and nurturing relationships is vital. Consider the following techniques:

1. **Consistent Communication**: Stay in touch with your connections through regular communication. Reach out with updates, greetings, or simply to check in.

2. **Reciprocity**: Offer your assistance and support when others in your network need it. The principle of reciprocity fosters strong, mutually beneficial relationships.

3. **Quality Over Quantity**: Focus on the quality of your relationships rather than the quantity. A smaller, more meaningful network is often more valuable than a large, superficial one.

4. **Acknowledgment and Gratitude**: Express appreciation for the people in your network.

5. **Shared Experiences**: Create opportunities for shared experiences with your connections. Going through experiences together can strengthen bonds.

6. **Conflict Resolution**: Address conflicts or misunderstandings promptly and diplomatically. Effective conflict resolution is essential for maintaining positive relationships.

7. **Celebrate Milestones**: Acknowledge and celebrate important milestones in the lives of your network members. Sharing in their joys and achievements strengthens connections.

Digital Networking Etiquette

In the digital age, online networking is increasingly important. Here are some essential digital networking etiquette tips:

1. **Professional Profile**: Maintain a professional and well-curated online profile. This includes a current photo, updated information, and appropriate content.

2. **Privacy Settings**: Adjust your privacy settings on social media to control what is visible to the public and your connections.

3. **Respectful Communication**: Be respectful and considerate in your online interactions. Avoid confrontational or offensive behavior.

4. **Avoid Spamming**: Refrain from spamming your connections with unsolicited messages or requests. Engage in meaningful conversations.

5. **Engage in Discussions**: Participate in online discussions and groups related to your interests and field. Contribute to meaningful conversations.

6. **Customized Connection Requests**: When sending connection requests, include a personalized message that explains your interest in connecting.

7. **Professional Email**: Use a professional email address for online networking.

Maintaining Boundaries

While cultivating networks is important, it's equally vital to maintain boundaries:

1. **Time Management**: Balance your networking activities with your other responsibilities. Avoid overcommitting to networking events or social gatherings.

2. **Respect Privacy**: Respect the privacy and boundaries of your connections. Avoid prying or intrusive questions and be mindful of sensitive topics.

3. **Professionalism**: Maintain professionalism in your professional networks. Avoid discussing highly personal matters or engaging in unprofessional behavior.

4. **Clear Expectations**: Set clear expectations in your relationships. Communicate openly about the nature and purpose of your connections.

5. **Consent**: Obtain consent before sharing or introducing your connections to others. Respect their choices in connecting with new individuals.

6. **Self-Care**: Prioritize self-care and personal well-being. Avoid overextending yourself in networking to the detriment of your own health and happiness.

Networking for Career Development

For those seeking career development, networking can be a powerful tool:

1. **Career Goals**: Define your career goals and objectives. Determine how your network can support your career path.

2. **Informational Interviews**: Conduct informational interviews with professionals in your desired field. Gather insights and advice for your career journey.

3. **Mentorship**: Seek out mentors who can guide you in your career development.

4. **Professional Development**: Attend workshops, webinars, and training programs related to your field. These events provide opportunities for networking and skill development.

5. **Job Searches**: Utilize your network to discover job opportunities. Personal referrals from connections can be highly valuable in the job market.

6. **Promote Your Expertise**: Share your expertise and insights through articles, presentations, or online content. Establishing yourself as an authority in your field can attract networking opportunities.

7. **Give Back**: Offer your assistance and support to others in your professional network.

Networking for Personal Growth

Networking can also significantly contribute to personal growth and development:

1. **Shared Interests**: Connect with individuals who share your personal interests and passions. These connections can provide opportunities for personal growth and enjoyment.

2. **Learning from Others**: Engage with people from diverse backgrounds and perspectives. Learning from others can broaden your horizons and enhance your personal development.

3. **Emotional Support**: Lean on your personal network for emotional support during challenging times. Friends and family can provide comfort and understanding.

4. **Collaborative Projects**: Collaborate on personal projects or hobbies with your network. Joint endeavors can lead to new skills and experiences.

5. **Wellness and Health**: Maintain connections with individuals who support your physical and mental well-being. Such connections can positively impact your health.

6. **Lifelong Learning**: Actively engage in lifelong learning by seeking knowledge and experiences through your personal network.

7. **Shared Experiences**: Create shared experiences with your connections, such as travel, adventures, or volunteering. Shared memories can enrich your personal growth.

Networking Challenges and Solutions

Networking isn't always smooth sailing, and challenges may arise. Here are some common challenges and their potential solutions:

1. **Time Constraints**: If you're pressed for time, focus on prioritizing the most valuable connections and events. Quality often outweighs quantity in networking.

2. **Introversion**: If you're an introvert, networking can be intimidating. Start with small, one-on-one interactions and gradually build your confidence.

3. **Overcome Rejection**: Not every connection will lead to a deep relationship. Be prepared for rejection and continue seeking out new opportunities.

4. **Maintaining Relationships**: As your network grows, it can be challenging to maintain all relationships. Regularly review

your connections and prioritize those that are most valuable to you.

5. **Conflict Resolution**: Address conflicts or misunderstandings with professionalism and diplomacy. Effective conflict resolution is essential for maintaining positive relationships.

6. **Online Etiquette**: Be mindful of online etiquette, ensuring that your digital interactions are respectful and professional.

7. **Balancing Personal and Professional**: Striking the right balance between personal and professional networks can be a challenge. Define clear boundaries and allocate time accordingly.

Conclusion

Cultivating and nurturing professional and personal networks is a lifelong endeavor that can significantly impact your career, personal growth, and overall well-being. By employing these techniques and strategies, you can build and maintain a robust network that provides opportunities, support, and enriching connections. Networking isn't just about who you know but also about how you engage with others, share experiences, and offer value to your connections. Whether you're focused on career development, personal growth, or a combination of both, effective networking can enhance your life in myriad ways.

Chapter 9: Personal Branding and Unique Personality

Defining Your Personal Brand

In today's interconnected and highly competitive world, personal branding has become an essential tool for achieving both professional and personal success. Your personal brand is the unique combination of your skills, experiences, values, and image that sets you apart from others. In this subsection, we will explore the importance of defining your personal brand and provide actionable steps to help you create a strong and authentic personal brand that aligns with your goals and aspirations.

The Significance of Personal Branding

Before we delve into the process of defining your personal brand, it's crucial to understand why personal branding is of great importance:

1. **Differentiation**: In a crowded marketplace, personal branding allows you to stand out. It emphasizes what makes you unique and distinguishes you from the competition.

2. **Credibility**: A well-defined personal brand can enhance your credibility and reputation. It provides a clear and consistent message to others about who you are and what you can offer.

3. **Career Advancement**: Personal branding is a powerful tool for career development. It can help you attract new opportunities, establish yourself as an expert, and advance in your chosen field.

4. **Alignment with Goals**: A strong personal brand aligns with your goals and aspirations. It helps you remain focused on the path you want to pursue and the impact you want to create.

5. **Authenticity**: Authentic personal branding encourages you to be true to yourself. It enables you to showcase your genuine strengths, values, and passions.

6. **Networking and Relationships**: A well-defined personal brand can help you build meaningful connections and relationships. It attracts like-minded individuals and opportunities that resonate with your brand.

Steps to Define Your Personal Brand

Defining your personal brand is a process that involves self-discovery, reflection, and strategic planning. Here are the steps to help you create a strong and authentic personal brand:

1. **Self-Discovery and Assessment**: Begin by conducting a self-assessment. Reflect on your skills, strengths, values, passions, and experiences. What sets you apart from others, and what are your unique qualities?

2. **Clarify Your Purpose**: Define your purpose and what you want to achieve. Identify your long-term goals and the impact you want to make in your personal and professional life.

3. **Target Audience**: Understand your target audience. Who are the people you want to connect with, influence, or serve? Tailor your brand to resonate with your intended audience.

4. **Craft Your Personal Brand Statement**: Create a concise and compelling personal brand statement. This statement should encapsulate who you are, what you do, who you do it for, and the value you provide.

5. **Identify Your Values and Principles**: Determine your core values and principles. Your personal brand should align with these beliefs and guide your actions and decisions.

6. **Establish Your Expertise**: Showcase your expertise and knowledge in your chosen field. Whether through education, experience, or personal passion, establish yourself as an authority in your domain.

7. **Visual and Online Presence**: Your online presence, including your website and social media profiles, plays a crucial role in personal branding. Ensure that your digital footprint reflects your personal brand consistently.

8. **Content Creation and Sharing**: Create and share content that reinforces your personal brand. This could include articles, blogs, videos, or social media posts that reflect your expertise and values.

9. **Build a Professional Network**: Connect with individuals and communities that align with your personal brand. Engage in networking opportunities that help you expand your reach.

10. **Feedback and Adaptation**: Seek feedback from peers, mentors, or trusted individuals to refine your personal brand. Be open to adaptation and growth as you evolve in your personal and professional journey.

11. **Maintain Consistency**: Consistency is key to personal branding. Ensure that your actions, communication, and behavior align with your defined personal brand.

12. **Tell Your Story**: Your personal brand is not just a list of skills; it's also the story you tell about yourself. Craft a narrative that engages others and connects with your brand.

13. **Monitor and Evaluate**: Continuously monitor your personal brand's effectiveness. Evaluate how well it resonates with your target audience and adjust your strategy as needed.

Authenticity in Personal Branding

Your brand should reflect your true self and resonate with your values. Authenticity not only attracts like-minded individuals but also helps you build trust and credibility with your audience.

To maintain authenticity in your personal branding:

- Showcase your unique strengths and skills.

- Share your experiences, including successes and challenges.

- Embrace vulnerability and admit when you don't have all the answers.

- Seek feedback and use it for growth and improvement.

Your personal brand is an ongoing journey, and as you evolve, your brand may evolve with you. Embrace this process as an opportunity for self-discovery and growth, and remember that authenticity is the key to a lasting and impactful personal brand.

Techniques for Leaving a Lasting Impression

Leaving a lasting impression is a powerful skill that can significantly impact your personal and professional life. Whether you're meeting new people, presenting to an audience, or simply engaging in conversations, the ability to make a memorable and positive impression is invaluable. In this subsection, we'll explore a range of techniques and strategies to help you leave a lasting impression that fosters connections, opens doors, and enhances your communication skills.

Why Leaving a Lasting Impression Matters

Before diving into the techniques, it's important to understand the significance of leaving a lasting impression:

1. **Memorability**: A lasting impression ensures that people remember you, your message, and your unique qualities long after your interaction.

2. **Building Relationships**: Creating a positive impression can lay the foundation for strong and lasting relationships in both personal and professional settings.

3. **Professional Advancement**: In the professional world, leaving a lasting impression can lead to opportunities, promotions, and career growth.

4. **Communication Efficacy**: A strong impression enhances your communication skills. It encourages active listening, engagement, and effective dialogue.

5. **Networking**: When you make a memorable impression, you're more likely to connect with influential individuals and expand your network.

Techniques for Leaving a Lasting Impression

1. **Active Listening**: One of the most powerful ways to leave a lasting impression is by being an active listener. Pay close attention to what the other person is saying, ask thoughtful questions, and show genuine interest in their thoughts and feelings.

2. **Engaging Eye Contact**: Maintain good eye contact during conversations. It conveys confidence, attentiveness, and sincerity. However, be mindful not to make the other person uncomfortable with prolonged staring.

3. **Warm and Confident Handshake**: A firm and confident handshake is often the first physical interaction in many social and professional encounters. It leaves a strong impression of self-assuredness and friendliness.

4. **Smile Sincerely**: A warm and sincere smile is a universal way to create a positive impression. It conveys approachability, positivity, and a genuine interest in the other person.

5. **Be Enthusiastic**: Show enthusiasm for the topic at hand and for the person you're engaging with. Enthusiasm is contagious and leaves a lasting impression of your passion and engagement.

6. **Use Positive Body Language**: Your body language, including posture and gestures, plays a significant role in impression-making. Maintain an open and welcoming posture to convey approachability.

7. **Show Empathy**: Empathizing with others, understanding their perspectives, and validating their feelings can create a deep and memorable connection.

8. **Tell Compelling Stories**: Storytelling is a powerful tool for leaving a lasting impression. Share relevant and engaging stories that convey your message and values effectively.

9. **Dress Appropriately**: Your attire and grooming communicate a lot about your professionalism and attention to detail. Dress appropriately for the occasion to leave a polished impression.

10. **Use Names**: Addressing people by their names is a simple yet effective way to leave a personalized and memorable impression.

11. **Express Gratitude**: Always express gratitude when it's appropriate. A thank-you note or a simple "thank you" in person can leave a lasting impression of your politeness and appreciation.

12. **Offer Value**: In professional interactions, offer value by sharing insights, resources, or solutions that can benefit the other person. This creates an impression of helpfulness and expertise.

13. **Customize Your Approach**: Tailor your communication style and message to the preferences and needs of your audience. Recognize and respect their individuality.

14. **Practice Positive Verbal Communication**: Use positive and affirming language. Avoid negative or critical remarks that can detract from the impression you want to create.

15. **Be Reliable**: Consistently follow through on your commitments and promises. Being reliable and dependable is a reliable way to leave a positive and lasting impression.

16. **Express Confidence**: Confidence in your abilities and ideas can be infectious. It demonstrates belief in yourself and your message.

17. **Respectful Disagreement**: If you disagree with someone, do so respectfully and constructively. The way you handle disagreements can leave a lasting impression of your maturity and professionalism.

18. **Follow Up**: After your initial interaction, follow up with a message or communication that shows your continued interest and commitment to the relationship.

19. **Maintain a Positive Attitude**: Positivity is attractive and memorable. Even in challenging situations, maintaining a positive attitude can leave a lasting impression of resilience and optimism.

20. **Be Authentic**: Above all, be true to yourself. Authenticity is a key factor in leaving a lasting impression. People are more likely to remember and connect with individuals who are genuine and true to their values.

Putting It into Practice

Leaving a lasting impression is not a one-size-fits-all endeavor. It involves adapting your approach to different situations and individuals. By applying these techniques and practicing them consistently, you can enhance your ability to make memorable impressions that lead to meaningful connections, opportunities, and positive relationships in both your personal and professional life. Remember that each interaction is an opportunity to make a lasting impression, so approach them with intention and authenticity.

Chapter 10: Mastering the Art of Influence

In the intricate tapestry of human interaction, influence stands as a powerful thread. The ability to influence others is not confined to charismatic leaders or salespeople; it's a skill that can be cultivated and mastered by anyone. Whether you're seeking to persuade, inspire, or lead, mastering the art of influence is a transformative skill that can shape your personal and professional life.

The Essence of Influence

Before we delve into the techniques and strategies for mastering influence, let's explore the essence of influence itself.

Understanding Influence

It's about persuading others to take a specific action, adopt a particular belief, or see things from your perspective. Influence can be both direct, such as when you're trying to convince someone to purchase a product, and indirect, where you aim to shape their thoughts or emotions.

The Impact of Influence

The impact of influence is vast and pervasive:

1. **Professional Advancement**: In the professional realm, influence is often the key to leadership, decision-making, and career progression. Those who can persuade and inspire tend to rise to influential positions.

2. **Personal Relationships**: In personal relationships, influence can foster deep connections, resolve conflicts, and strengthen bonds with loved ones.

3. **Leadership and Change**: Effective leaders are those who can influence their teams to achieve common goals. Change management and innovation often hinge on leaders' capacity to influence.

4. **Sales and Marketing**: The worlds of sales and marketing rely heavily on influence. Marketers use strategies to influence consumers' choices, while salespeople aim to persuade customers to make a purchase.

5. **Public Speaking and Presentations**: Captivating public speakers and presenters are adept at wielding influence to engage their audiences and convey their messages effectively.

The Psychology of Influence

To master the art of influence, it's essential to delve into the psychology behind it. Understanding the psychological principles that underpin influence strategies can empower you to use them more effectively.

Reciprocity

Reciprocity is a fundamental principle of influence. It's the idea that people tend to reciprocate when someone provides them with something of value. To use reciprocity in influence, you can offer assistance, information, or resources before seeking anything in return. This creates a sense of indebtedness and a willingness to cooperate.

Social Proof

Social proof is the phenomenon where people look to the behavior of others to guide their actions and decisions. When they see that others are doing something, they are more inclined to follow suit. You can leverage social proof by highlighting endorsements, testimonials, or statistics that demonstrate the popularity or success of your idea or product.

Commitment and Consistency

People tend to align their behavior with their past commitments and actions. If you can get someone to make a small commitment or take a small step in a particular direction, they are more likely to follow through with a larger commitment or action in the same direction. For influence, you can start by asking for small, manageable commitments that are in line with your ultimate goal.

Authority

The authority principle emphasizes that people are more likely to comply with requests from authoritative figures or credible sources. When you're seeking to influence others, establishing your expertise, credentials, or credibility can enhance your persuasive power.

Liking

People are more inclined to be influenced by those they like or feel a connection with. Building rapport, being friendly, and finding common ground can significantly boost your ability to influence others. This principle can also be applied in sales and marketing, where building a personal connection can lead to higher conversion rates.

Scarcity

Scarcity is the concept that people place a higher value on opportunities, products, or information that are limited in availability. To use scarcity in influence, you can emphasize the exclusivity or limited quantity of what you're offering. This can create a sense of urgency and motivate others to act quickly.

Strategies for Mastering Influence

Now that we've explored the psychology of influence, let's delve into strategies for mastering the art of influence.

Know Your Audience

Effective influence begins with understanding your audience. Consider their needs, values, and beliefs. Tailor your approach to align with what resonates with them.

Build Trust

Trust is the foundation of influence.

Establish Credibility

Credibility enhances your influence. Demonstrate your expertise and experience in the relevant area, and cite credible sources when making your case.

Be Confident

Confidence can be influential. Speak with conviction and assurance, but avoid coming across as arrogant. Confidence instills faith in your message.

Craft a Compelling Message

Your message should be clear, concise, and persuasive. Highlight the benefits and address potential concerns. Use storytelling and emotional appeals to make your message memorable.

Use Persuasive Techniques

Employ the psychological principles of influence, such as reciprocity, social proof, commitment, authority, liking, and scarcity, to make your case more compelling.

Be Empathetic

Empathy is a powerful tool in influence. Show that you understand and care about the concerns and needs of others. Empathetic listening and responses can build strong connections.

Be Flexible

Flexibility is crucial in influence. Be willing to adapt your approach and message based on the feedback and reactions you receive. Flexibility allows you to navigate different personalities and situations effectively.

Overcome Objections

Anticipate and address objections proactively. Understand the potential concerns or resistance your audience may have and provide well-thought-out responses.

Build Consistency

Create consistency in your messages and actions. People are more likely to be influenced by those who have a track record of being consistent and reliable.

Provide Value

Offer value to your audience. Whether it's in the form of information, solutions, or support, demonstrating how your influence benefits others is a compelling strategy.

Be Patient

Influence may not yield immediate results. It often requires patience and persistence. Don't be discouraged if your initial efforts do not lead to the desired outcome.

Seek Feedback

Feedback is invaluable for fine-tuning your influence strategies. Solicit feedback from others to understand how you can improve your approach.

Practice Ethical Influence

While influence can be powerful, it's important to use it ethically and responsibly. Avoid manipulative tactics or tactics that exploit vulnerabilities.

Real-Life Examples of Influence

To illustrate the power of influence, let's explore real-life examples where influence played a pivotal role:

1. **Martin Luther King Jr.**: Through his powerful speeches and commitment to nonviolent protest, Martin Luther King Jr. influenced the civil rights movement, bringing about significant social change.

2. **Steve Jobs**: Steve Jobs' ability to influence consumer behavior and industry trends through innovative product launches and marketing strategies is legendary.

3. **Oprah Winfrey**: Oprah's influence extends across various domains, from media to philanthropy. Her empathetic and relatable communication style has resonated with millions.

4. **Nelson Mandela**: Nelson Mandela's influence was instrumental in ending apartheid in South Africa. His commitment to reconciliation and justice influenced a nation.

5. **Malala Yousafzai**: Malala's advocacy for girls' education, even after surviving a life-threatening attack, has influenced international policies and attitudes toward female education.

Application of Influence in Daily Life

Influence isn't limited to grand movements or public figures; it's a skill that can be applied in our everyday lives:

1. **Family Dynamics**: Influencing family members can foster stronger bonds and resolve conflicts.

2. **Workplace Relationships**: Effective influence can lead to better collaboration, leadership, and career advancement.

3. **Negotiations**: Influential negotiation skills can result in favorable agreements and resolutions.

4. **Community Engagement**: Influencing your community can lead to positive changes and impact local issues.

5. **Social Advocacy**: Advocating for social or environmental causes often relies on the power of influence to mobilize support.

Cultivating Your Influence

It involves continuous learning, practice, and self-reflection. As you navigate the various aspects of your personal and professional life, remember that influence is not about manipulation but about fostering positive change and building meaningful connections. It's a skill that, when honed ethically and effectively, can lead to personal and collective growth.

In the following chapters, we will explore specific areas where influence is essential, from effective leadership to navigating conflicts and inspiring others. The journey to mastering influence is an exciting one, and it's one that can have a profound impact on your life and the lives of those you connect with.

Chapter 11: The Power of Effective Listening

In a world where communication is often associated with speaking, the often-overlooked skill of listening holds immense power. Effective listening is not merely hearing words but truly understanding the message, emotions, and intentions behind them. It's a skill that can transform relationships, boost professional success, and enhance personal growth. In this chapter, we will explore the profound influence of effective listening and the strategies to harness its power.

The Essence of Effective Listening

Before we delve into the strategies for effective listening, let's understand the essence of this crucial skill.

What Is Effective Listening?

Effective listening is an active process of receiving, interpreting, and responding to spoken or unspoken messages. It goes beyond hearing words; it involves engaging with the speaker's thoughts, emotions, and perspectives. Effective listening is about providing undivided attention, empathy, and genuine interest in the speaker.

The Impact of Effective Listening

Effective listening can have a transformative impact in various aspects of life:

1. **Improved Relationships**: It fosters stronger, more meaningful connections in personal and professional relationships. Being truly heard and understood creates trust and intimacy.

2. **Conflict Resolution**: Effective listening is a cornerstone of conflict resolution. It allows parties to express their concerns and perspectives while feeling valued.

3. **Enhanced Communication**: It leads to more precise and effective communication. When listeners grasp the full message, the risk of misunderstandings and miscommunications diminishes.

4. **Leadership**: Effective leaders are skilled listeners. They understand their team's needs, provide guidance, and inspire based on a deep understanding of their followers.

5. **Career Advancement**: In the workplace, listening skills can boost career advancement. It helps in building strong professional relationships, understanding colleagues' needs, and contributing to effective teamwork.

The Psychology of Effective Listening

To harness the power of effective listening, it's essential to understand the psychological foundations that make it so impactful.

Validation and Empathy

Listening is a fundamental way to validate and express empathy. Empathy—understanding and sharing another person's feelings—is a core component of effective listening.

Trust and Rapport

Effective listening builds trust and rapport. When people believe that their thoughts and feelings are valued, they are more likely to trust and connect with the listener.

Conflict Resolution

In conflict situations, effective listening is a critical tool. It allows individuals to express their concerns, and it often paves the way for constructive solutions and compromises.

Persuasion

Effective listening can be persuasive. When people feel heard, they are more receptive to the listener's ideas and suggestions.

Relationship Building

Effective listening is a key factor in building and maintaining relationships. It deepens connections, increases intimacy, and strengthens bonds.

Strategies for Effective Listening

Let's explore strategies for mastering the art of effective listening.

Be Fully Present

Effective listening begins with being fully present in the moment.

Maintain Eye Contact

Eye contact signals your engagement and attentiveness. It conveys that you are genuinely interested in what the speaker is saying.

Avoid Interrupting

Use Non-Verbal Cues

Non-verbal cues, such as nodding, smiling, and mirroring the speaker's emotions, can convey your active listening and understanding.

Ask Open-Ended Questions

These questions invite deeper discussion and reflection.

Reflect and Paraphrase

Reflect the speaker's thoughts and feelings by paraphrasing what they've said. This demonstrates that you are actively processing their message.

Empathize

Understanding their perspective fosters trust and connection.

Practice Mindfulness

Mindfulness can enhance your listening skills by promoting active awareness and non-judgmental attention to the speaker.

Be Patient

Effective listening requires patience. Allow the speaker to express themselves fully without rushing or pushing for a response.

Suspend Judgment

Suspend judgment while listening. Avoid forming conclusions or opinions until the speaker has fully shared their perspective.

Real-Life Examples of Effective Listening

To illustrate the power of effective listening, let's explore real-life examples where it played a pivotal role:

1. **Marriage Counseling**: In couples' therapy, effective listening helps partners understand each other's concerns, rebuild trust, and work toward healthier relationships.

2. **Conflict Resolution**: Mediators use effective listening to facilitate dialogue between conflicting parties, enabling them to express their grievances and reach solutions.

3. **Mentorship**: Mentors actively listen to their mentees, offering guidance and support based on a deep understanding of their goals and challenges.

4. **Therapeutic Settings**: Therapists rely on effective listening to help clients explore their thoughts and emotions, promoting healing and personal growth.

5. **Effective Leadership**: Effective leaders listen to their team members' concerns, needs, and feedback. This fosters a

positive work environment and enables informed decision-making.

Application of Effective Listening in Daily Life

Effective listening is a skill that can be applied in numerous areas of daily life:

1. **Personal Relationships**: Active listening enhances intimacy and trust in personal relationships. It fosters healthier, more connected partnerships.

2. **Parenting**: Effective listening is valuable in parenting, as it enables parents to understand their children's feelings and concerns.

3. **Customer Service**: In customer service roles, effective listening is critical to understanding customers' needs and resolving issues.

4. **Conflict Resolution**: Whether in familial disputes or workplace conflicts, effective listening is a powerful tool for reaching resolutions.

5. **Leadership**: Effective leaders are skilled listeners. They create strong teams and make well-informed decisions based on their understanding of their team members.

Cultivating Effective Listening

Mastering the art of effective listening is a continuous journey of self-awareness and skill development. As you navigate the various aspects of your life, remember that effective listening is not passive but an active choice to engage, empathize, and connect with others. It's a skill that can deeply influence the quality of your relationships, the success of your career, and the overall richness of your life. In the following chapters, we will further explore how effective listening plays a pivotal role in leadership, conflict resolution, and inspiring others.

Chapter 12: Navigating Difficult Conversations

Life is replete with conversations that are not always easy or comfortable. Whether you need to address conflicts, deliver unwelcome news, or discuss sensitive topics, navigating difficult conversations is an essential skill. In this chapter, we will delve into the art of handling challenging dialogues with grace, ensuring that they lead to productive outcomes rather than conflict and tension.

The Complexity of Difficult Conversations

Before we explore strategies for navigating difficult conversations, let's understand the complexity of these interactions.

What Makes Conversations Difficult?

Difficult conversations can encompass a range of scenarios:

1. **Conflict Resolution**: Addressing conflicts, disagreements, and disputes, whether at work or in personal relationships.

2. **Delivering Feedback**: Providing constructive criticism or negative feedback, which can be challenging to do without causing defensiveness.

3. **Sharing Bad News**: Communicating difficult or distressing news to others, such as layoffs, illness, or personal setbacks.

4. **Discussing Sensitive Topics**: Engaging in conversations about sensitive subjects like money, religion, politics, or personal boundaries.

5. **Apologies and Forgiveness**: Apologizing or seeking forgiveness for mistakes or transgressions can be emotionally charged.

The Stakes of Difficult Conversations

Difficult conversations can have significant consequences, both positive and negative. They can lead to resolution, improved understanding, and strengthened relationships, but mishandling them can result in damaged connections, unresolved issues, and heightened conflict.

Strategies for Navigating Difficult Conversations

Let's explore strategies for effectively navigating difficult conversations:

Preparation

Define Your Purpose

Before entering a difficult conversation, clarify your purpose and objectives. What do you hope to achieve? This will guide your approach and keep the conversation on track.

Self-Reflection

Take time for self-reflection to understand your feelings and perspectives. Recognize any biases or emotions that may impact the conversation.

Create a Safe Environment

Establish a safe and conducive environment for the conversation. Choose a private, quiet space and ensure you won't be interrupted.

Active Listening

Listening is paramount in difficult conversations. Show empathy and understanding.

Use "I" Statements

Frame your statements using "I" language to express your feelings and perspective without assigning blame. For example, say, "I felt hurt when..." instead of "You hurt me when..."

Avoid Accusations

Steer clear of accusatory language or blame. Instead, focus on the specific actions, behaviors, or situations that need to be addressed.

Find Common Ground

Seek areas of agreement or common ground with the other person. Starting with shared perspectives can pave the way for productive discussion.

Ask Open-Ended Questions

This can lead to deeper insights and mutual understanding.

Maintain Emotional Control

Stay composed and in control of your emotions. Even in emotionally charged conversations, emotional control can help keep the dialogue constructive.

Stay Solution-Focused

Keep the conversation centered on finding solutions and resolutions.

Offer a Path Forward

In challenging conversations, provide a way forward. Suggest potential solutions or steps to address the issues at hand.

Be Empathetic

Show empathy toward the other person's feelings and perspectives. Recognize that they may also be experiencing discomfort.

Acknowledge Emotions

Emotions often play a significant role in difficult conversations.

Set Boundaries

If the conversation becomes unproductive or disrespectful, it's essential to set boundaries. Politely but firmly communicate your need for respectful dialogue.

Real-Life Examples of Navigating Difficult Conversations

To illustrate the art of navigating difficult conversations, let's explore real-life examples where effective communication led to resolution and understanding:

1. **Workplace Conflicts**: HR professionals and managers often mediate workplace conflicts, helping employees communicate effectively to resolve issues.

2. **Family Disputes**: Family therapists assist in navigating and resolving family disputes, whether they involve parenting, inheritance, or relationships.

3. **Relationship Counseling**: Relationship counselors help couples have productive conversations to address issues and improve their relationships.

4. **Performance Reviews**: Managers conduct performance reviews with employees, offering feedback and setting goals for improvement.

5. **Medical Conversations**: Healthcare professionals navigate difficult conversations with patients, such as discussing diagnoses, treatment options, and end-of-life care.

Application of Navigating Difficult Conversations in Daily Life

The ability to navigate difficult conversations is valuable in various aspects of daily life:

1. **Personal Relationships**: Addressing conflicts, misunderstandings, and sensitive topics is essential for maintaining healthy and loving relationships.

2. **Workplace Communication**: Managers and colleagues often need to conduct challenging conversations, such as performance evaluations, project disagreements, or addressing behavioral issues.

3. **Parenting**: Parents navigate difficult conversations with their children, addressing discipline, boundaries, and life challenges.

4. **Friendships**: Difficult conversations can arise in friendships, requiring open and honest communication to resolve issues.

5. **Community and Advocacy**: Engaging in discussions about social issues, politics, or community concerns may necessitate navigating difficult conversations with empathy and understanding.

Cultivating Effective Conversation Navigation

Navigating difficult conversations is an art that requires practice and self-awareness. When approached with care and respect, challenging dialogues can lead to resolution, understanding, and improved relationships. As you apply these strategies in your own life, you will find that difficult conversations can become opportunities for growth and transformation, both personally and in your interactions with others. In the following chapters, we will delve into topics such as conflict resolution, inspiring others, and leadership, where the skills of navigating difficult conversations play a pivotal role.

Chapter 13: Building Trust and Credibility

Welcome to a pivotal chapter that holds the key to transforming the way you connect with others. In this chapter, we'll explore the profound art of building trust and credibility, a skill that can revolutionize your personal and professional life. It's a journey that begins with understanding the vital role trust plays in human relationships and ends with the recognition that credibility is the currency of influence.

The Foundation of Trust

Before we dive into the strategies for building trust and credibility, let's uncover the very essence of trust itself.

Trust: The Heart of Human Connection

Trust is the linchpin of human connection. It's the unwavering belief in someone's reliability, integrity, and intentions. Trust forms the foundation of strong relationships, whether they're personal or professional. It's the glue that binds friendships, partnerships, and successful collaborations.

The Power of Trust

Trust carries immense power:

1. **Strengthened Relationships**: Trust deepens bonds and fosters genuine connections, helping relationships thrive.

2. **Enhanced Communication**: Trust opens the gates to honest and transparent communication, facilitating meaningful dialogue.

3. **Effective Leadership**: Leaders who are trusted inspire loyalty and commitment in their teams.

4. **Professional Success**: In the professional realm, trust is the bedrock of reputation, leading to opportunities, partnerships, and career advancement.

5. **Conflict Resolution**: Trust enables the resolution of conflicts and disputes with a higher likelihood of achieving mutual understanding.

Strategies for Building Trust and Credibility

Now, let's embark on the journey of mastering the art of building trust and credibility.

Authenticity

Embrace Authenticity

Authenticity is your ticket to trust. Be genuine, honest, and true to your values and principles.

Vulnerability

Openness and vulnerability are powerful trust builders. Sharing your thoughts, feelings, and even your fears can create a sense of mutual understanding and trust.

Consistency

Consistency is the cornerstone of credibility:

Keep Your Word

Consistently following through on your promises and commitments is a fundamental aspect of building trust. It demonstrates reliability and integrity.

Reliability

Reliability is a trust magnet. Being consistent in your actions and responses fosters trust because others know they can rely on you.

Empathy

Empathy is the bridge to trust:

Understand Others

Empathy is about truly understanding the thoughts and emotions of others.

Compassion

Compassion is a genuine expression of empathy. Show that you care about the well-being of others, and they will trust your intentions.

Communication

Effective communication is a trust accelerator:

Open Dialogue

Foster open and transparent communication. Share your thoughts, expectations, and concerns, and encourage others to do the same.

Active Listening

By listening attentively and demonstrating understanding, you build trust with your words and your ears.

Reliability

Reliability is the bedrock of credibility:

Deliver on Promises

Consistently delivering on your promises and commitments enhances your reputation for reliability.

Honesty

Honesty is the currency of credibility. Be honest in your words and actions, and your credibility will soar.

Competence

Credibility is closely tied to competence:

Continuous Learning

Commit to lifelong learning and self-improvement. Competence is not static, and by continuously improving your skills, you bolster your credibility.

Expertise

Becoming an expert in your field strengthens your credibility. Your knowledge and expertise become valuable assets that others can trust.

Accountability

Accountability is a trust-preserver:

Take Responsibility

Accountability builds trust by showing integrity and a commitment to improvement.

Follow Through

Consistently following through on your commitments is a demonstration of your accountability.

Real-Life Examples of Building Trust and Credibility

Let's draw inspiration from real-life examples where individuals and organizations have mastered the art of building trust and credibility:

1. **Elon Musk and SpaceX**: Through groundbreaking achievements and consistent innovation, Elon Musk and SpaceX have earned the trust and credibility of the space exploration community.

2. **Warren Buffett**: Renowned investor Warren Buffett is trusted by millions due to his transparency, reliability, and expertise in the world of finance.

3. **Nelson Mandela**: Nelson Mandela's unwavering commitment to justice and reconciliation earned him the trust and credibility of an entire nation.

4. **Consumer Brands**: Brands like Apple and Google have built trust and credibility through their consistent delivery of quality products and services.

5. **Mentorship**: Trusted mentors and teachers inspire confidence and trust in their students by providing guidance and support.

Application of Building Trust and Credibility in Daily Life

The art of building trust and credibility is not confined to public figures or businesses. It's a skill that can be applied in various aspects of daily life:

1. **Friendships**: Trust is the heart of meaningful friendships. Being authentic, reliable, and empathetic strengthens bonds.

2. **Parenting**: Parents who build trust and credibility with their children foster open communication and mutual understanding.

3. **Workplace**: Trust and credibility are essential in the workplace, impacting career advancement, team collaboration, and professional relationships.

4. **Leadership**: Effective leaders build trust and credibility, inspiring loyalty and commitment in their teams.

5. **Community Engagement**: Building trust and credibility within communities is vital for effective advocacy, collaboration, and social change.

Cultivating Trust and Credibility

The path to building trust and credibility is a journey of self-discovery and conscious choices. It's about embracing authenticity, consistency, empathy, and effective communication. As you navigate your personal and professional interactions, remember that trust and credibility are not just lofty ideals but attainable skills that can transform your relationships and your life. In the following chapters, we'll delve into more topics, including conflict resolution, inspiring others, and leadership, where the trust and credibility you've cultivated will play a pivotal role.

Chapter 14: Harnessing the Psychology of Communication

Welcome to a chapter that delves deep into the fascinating world of the human psyche and the intricate mechanisms that govern our communication. Understanding the psychology of communication is the key to mastering the art of influence, persuasion, and effective connection. In this chapter, we'll explore the psychological principles that shape our communication and provide you with valuable insights and strategies to navigate conversations with greater impact.

The Psychology of Communication

Before we embark on this enlightening journey, let's explore the very essence of the psychology of communication.

Communication as a Psychological Process

Communication is not merely an exchange of words; it's a complex psychological process. It involves the transmission of thoughts, emotions, and intentions from one mind to another. To become a master communicator, you must grasp the psychology that underlies this process.

The Power of Perception

Perception is at the core of communication. How we perceive information, individuals, and situations shapes our responses and decisions. Understanding perception is the first step in harnessing the psychology of communication.

Psychological Principles of Communication

Now, let's delve into the psychological principles that govern communication:

Persuasion and Influence

The Art of Persuasion

Persuasion is a powerful psychological tool. It involves convincing others to adopt a particular belief, attitude, or action. Whether you're persuading in a sales pitch, a negotiation, or an everyday conversation, understanding the principles of persuasion is essential.

The Psychology of Influence

Influence is the subtle art of shaping others' behavior and decisions. By tapping into psychological triggers, you can become a more influential communicator. We'll explore the psychology behind influential communication and the factors that drive human decisions.

Cognitive Biases

Cognitive biases are the quirks of human thinking that impact our decision-making and perceptions. By recognizing these biases, you can navigate communication more effectively:

Confirmation Bias

People tend to seek and interpret information that confirms their existing beliefs. Understand how confirmation bias affects communication and how to counteract it.

Anchoring Bias

Anchoring bias occurs when individuals rely heavily on the first piece of information they receive. Discover how to use anchoring to your advantage in negotiations and persuasion.

Availability Heuristic

Learn how to leverage this bias to make your message more memorable.

Emotional Intelligence

Emotional intelligence is the ability to recognize, understand, and manage your own emotions and the emotions of others.

Empathy

Empathy is a core component of emotional intelligence. By understanding others' emotions and demonstrating empathy, you can create stronger connections and resolve conflicts.

Emotional Regulation

Emotional regulation allows you to remain composed and responsive in emotionally charged situations. It's a valuable skill for navigating conversations with grace and impact.

Strategies for Applying Psychological Insights

Now, let's explore practical strategies for applying psychological insights to your communication:

Framing

By using framing techniques, you can shape the narrative of a conversation and guide others toward your desired outcome.

Storytelling

Storytelling is a potent tool for engaging and persuading others. By understanding the psychology of storytelling, you can craft compelling narratives that resonate with your audience.

Body Language

Non-verbal communication, including body language and facial expressions, conveys powerful psychological cues. Learn how to read and use body language to enhance your communication.

Active Listening

Active listening is not only about hearing words but also about understanding the underlying emotions and intentions. By practicing active listening, you can build trust and rapport in your conversations.

Mirroring

Mirroring involves matching the body language and speech patterns of the person you're communicating with. This subtle technique can foster a sense of connection and rapport.

Use of Language

The words you choose and the language you use can significantly impact how your message is received. Learn to use language effectively to influence and persuade.

Behavioral Nudges

Behavioral nudges are subtle prompts that guide people toward specific actions. By implementing nudges in your communication, you can influence decision-making and behavior.

Real-Life Examples of Psychological Communication

To illustrate the power of psychological communication, let's explore real-life examples where individuals and organizations have harnessed psychological insights to achieve their goals:

1. **Marketing and Advertising**: Companies use psychological principles to craft persuasive advertisements that drive consumer behavior.

2. **Political Campaigns**: Political strategists employ psychological tactics to influence voters and shape public opinion.

3. **Negotiations**: Skilled negotiators leverage psychological insights to reach favorable agreements and outcomes.

4. **Therapeutic Settings**: Therapists and counselors use psychological communication techniques to help clients navigate challenges and achieve personal growth.

5. **Leadership**: Effective leaders understand the psychology of motivation and use it to inspire and lead their teams.

Application of Psychological Communication in Daily Life

The principles of psychological communication can be applied in numerous aspects of daily life:

1. **Personal Relationships**: Understanding cognitive biases, emotional intelligence, and persuasion can enhance your personal connections and resolve conflicts.

2. **Workplace**: Applying psychological insights in the workplace can boost your leadership, negotiation, and collaboration skills.

3. **Parenting**: Psychological communication techniques can be valuable in parenting, fostering open dialogue and understanding.

4. **Community Engagement**: When engaging with your community or advocating for social change, psychological communication can be a powerful tool.

5. **Self-Improvement**: Applying these principles to self-improvement can help you set and achieve personal goals.

Cultivating Psychological Communication

Mastering the psychology of communication is an ongoing journey of self-awareness and skill development. As you navigate the various aspects of your life, remember that communication is not just about words; it's about understanding and influencing the thoughts, emotions, and decisions of others. The knowledge and strategies you gain in this chapter will empower you to navigate conversations with greater impact and effectiveness. In the following chapters, we'll further explore topics such as conflict resolution, inspiring others, and leadership, where the psychology of communication plays a pivotal role. Get ready for more transformative insights and practical guidance.

Chapter 15: Connecting in a Digital World: Online Communication

As we dive into the digital age, online communication has become an integral part of our lives. The ability to connect with others across vast distances, share ideas, and collaborate in the virtual realm has revolutionized the way we interact. In this chapter, we'll explore the intricacies of online communication, providing you with valuable insights and strategies to navigate the digital landscape effectively.

The Evolution of Online Communication

Before we delve into the strategies for effective online communication, let's take a moment to understand the evolution of this revolutionary mode of interaction.

From Text-Based Forums to Multimedia Conversations

Online communication has come a long way. It began with text-based forums and email, eventually evolving into dynamic multimedia conversations. Today, we communicate through text, images, videos, voice messages, and real-time video chats. Understanding this evolution is essential for navigating the diverse channels available to us.

The Impact on Personal and Professional Life

Online communication has transformed both personal and professional aspects of our lives. It has redefined how we socialize, learn, work, and conduct business. Recognizing the profound impact it has on our daily routines is crucial for making the most of the digital world.

Strategies for Effective Online Communication

Now, let's explore practical strategies for mastering online communication:

Digital Etiquette

Netiquette: Online Etiquette

Netiquette, or online etiquette, is essential for fostering respectful and productive online interactions. Learn the dos and don'ts of digital communication, including the importance of tone and politeness in your messages.

Email Communication

Email remains a prominent mode of professional communication. Discover how to compose effective and concise emails, including tips on subject lines, formatting, and follow-ups.

Social Media Interaction

Leveraging Social Media

Social media platforms provide opportunities for personal and professional connection. Understand the best practices for engaging with your network, including crafting compelling profiles, posting relevant content, and connecting with others.

Privacy and Security

Online security is paramount. Learn how to protect your personal and professional information, recognize phishing attempts, and ensure your online presence is secure.

Video Conferencing

Mastering Video Meetings

Video conferencing has become a staple in professional and personal settings. Enhance your video meeting skills, including camera presence, lighting, and engagement techniques.

Webinars and Virtual Events

Participating in webinars and virtual events offers unique networking opportunities. Explore strategies for effective participation, from asking insightful questions to connecting with presenters and attendees.

Chat and Messaging Apps

Effective Messaging

Messaging apps facilitate quick and convenient communication. Learn how to maintain clarity and professionalism in your text-based exchanges, including managing group chats and using emojis and gifs appropriately.

Online Networking

Building Digital Networks

Online platforms like LinkedIn provide opportunities for networking. Discover strategies for creating a compelling online presence, connecting with peers, and engaging in meaningful conversations.

Collaboration Tools

Remote Collaboration

Collaboration tools are essential for remote work and project management. Understand how to leverage these platforms for efficient teamwork, document sharing, and task tracking.

Online Learning

Digital Education

Online learning has become a standard mode of education. Explore strategies for staying engaged and productive in online courses, including time management and active participation in virtual classrooms.

Real-Life Examples of Effective Online Communication

To illustrate the power of effective online communication, let's explore real-life examples where individuals and organizations have harnessed digital communication to achieve their goals:

1. **Remote Work**: In the wake of the COVID-19 pandemic, countless professionals have adapted to remote work, effectively communicating and collaborating with their teams through digital tools.

2. **Virtual Events**: The proliferation of virtual events, such as conferences, trade shows, and concerts, showcases the power of online communication in reaching a global audience.

3. **Online Education**: Educational institutions and e-learning platforms have embraced online communication to provide students with engaging and effective learning experiences.

4. **Social Media Influencers**: Social media influencers have mastered the art of online communication to build and engage their digital audiences.

5. **Customer Support**: Many businesses offer customer support through online chats, ensuring quick and efficient assistance for their customers.

Application of Online Communication in Daily Life

The principles of effective online communication can be applied in various aspects of daily life:

1. **Personal Relationships**: Strengthen your personal connections by communicating effectively with friends and family through digital channels.

2. **Remote Work**: Master online communication for professional success in remote work settings, from video meetings to email correspondence.

3. **Entrepreneurship**: Entrepreneurs and small business owners can harness the power of online communication for marketing, networking, and client interactions.

4. **Education**: Students of all ages can optimize their online learning experiences through effective communication and engagement.

5. **Online Advocacy**: Engage in online advocacy and social causes by using digital platforms to raise awareness and mobilize support.

Cultivating Effective Online Communication

Mastering online communication is an ongoing journey of adaptation and skill development. As you navigate the diverse digital channels available to you, remember that online communication offers limitless possibilities for connection and collaboration. The knowledge and strategies you gain in this chapter will empower you to communicate effectively in the digital realm. In the following chapters, we'll delve into topics like conflict resolution, inspiring others, and leadership, where online communication skills play a pivotal role. Get ready for more transformative insights and practical guidance.

Chapter 16: Emotional Intelligence and Communication

Welcome to a chapter that explores the profound relationship between emotional intelligence and effective communication. Emotional intelligence, often abbreviated as EI or EQ, plays a pivotal role in how we connect with others, understand their emotions, and navigate complex interpersonal dynamics. In this chapter, we'll delve into the intricate interplay of emotional intelligence and communication, equipping you with the knowledge and strategies to enhance your ability to connect on a deeper level.

Understanding Emotional Intelligence

Before we explore the strategies for combining emotional intelligence and communication, let's take a moment to understand the fundamental concepts of EI.

What Is Emotional Intelligence?

Emotional intelligence refers to the ability to recognize, understand, manage, and influence your own emotions and the emotions of others.

The Four Components of Emotional Intelligence

Emotional intelligence comprises four essential components:

1. **Self-Awareness**: The ability to recognize and understand your emotions, including their causes and impact on your thoughts and behavior.

2. **Self-Regulation**: The capacity to manage and control your emotions, ensuring they don't overwhelm your decision-making and communication.

3. **Social Awareness**: The skill of perceiving and understanding the emotions of others, including their unspoken cues and feelings.

4. **Relationship Management**: The capability to use your emotional awareness to navigate interpersonal relationships effectively.

The Role of Emotional Intelligence in Communication

Now, let's explore how emotional intelligence influences communication:

Empathy

It's the cornerstone of effective communication, allowing you to connect on a deeper level and respond to the emotional needs of those you communicate with.

Self-Regulation

Self-regulation is essential for managing your emotions during conversations. It enables you to remain composed and thoughtful, even in emotionally charged situations, fostering effective and respectful communication.

Social Awareness

Social awareness, another aspect of emotional intelligence, involves recognizing and understanding the emotions of those around you. It allows you to interpret non-verbal cues, such as body language and tone of voice, which are vital for successful communication.

Relationship Management

The ability to manage relationships is at the core of emotional intelligence. It involves using your emotional awareness to inspire, influence, and navigate complex interpersonal dynamics in your communication.

Strategies for Enhancing Emotional Intelligence in Communication

Now, let's explore practical strategies for combining emotional intelligence and communication:

Self-Awareness

Recognize Your Emotions

To enhance self-awareness, pay attention to your emotions during conversations. Recognize what you're feeling, why you're feeling that way, and how it influences your communication.

Reflect on Your Responses

After interactions, take time to reflect on your responses and their emotional impact. Consider whether your emotional reactions were appropriate and if there are areas for improvement.

Self-Regulation

Manage Emotional Triggers

Identify your emotional triggers, the situations or topics that provoke strong emotional reactions. Develop strategies to manage these triggers and maintain emotional composure during communication.

Practice Mindfulness

Mindfulness techniques can help you stay present and in control during conversations. Engage in practices like deep breathing and meditation to enhance self-regulation.

Empathy

Listen Actively

Active listening is a powerful tool for practicing empathy. Pay close attention to what others are saying and show that you understand their emotions and perspectives.

Ask Open-Ended Questions

Encourage others to share their feelings and thoughts by asking open-ended questions that go beyond yes or no answers. This allows for more meaningful and empathetic conversations.

Social Awareness

Read Non-Verbal Cues

Become adept at reading non-verbal cues during communication. Pay attention to body language, facial expressions, and tone of voice to grasp the emotions of others.

Practice Perspective-Taking

Try to see the situation from their perspective, which enhances your social awareness and empathy.

Relationship Management

Adapt Your Communication Style

Recognize that different situations and individuals may require different communication styles. Flexibility in your approach allows you to manage relationships effectively.

Resolve Conflicts with Empathy

In conflicts, approach the resolution with empathy. Show understanding of the other person's feelings and work toward mutually beneficial solutions.

Real-Life Examples of Emotional Intelligence in Communication

To illustrate the power of emotional intelligence in communication, let's explore real-life examples where individuals have harnessed their EI to achieve their goals:

1. **Leadership**: Effective leaders demonstrate emotional intelligence by understanding and responding to the emotions

of their team members. They use this understanding to motivate, inspire, and lead effectively.

2. **Customer Service**: Customer service professionals use empathy and emotional intelligence to connect with customers, understand their concerns, and provide satisfactory solutions.

3. **Negotiation**: Skilled negotiators leverage emotional intelligence to establish rapport, understand the needs of the other party, and reach favorable agreements.

4. **Conflict Resolution**: Conflict resolution experts use empathy and emotional awareness to mediate disputes and guide parties toward resolution.

5. **Mentoring and Coaching**: Mentors and coaches use emotional intelligence to support and guide their mentees, helping them grow personally and professionally.

Application of Emotional Intelligence in Communication in Daily Life

The principles of emotional intelligence and communication can be applied in various aspects of daily life:

1. **Personal Relationships**: Enhance your personal connections and resolve conflicts by practicing empathy and emotional awareness in your interactions with family and friends.

2. **Workplace**: Leverage emotional intelligence for professional success in leadership, teamwork, and effective communication with colleagues and supervisors.

3. **Parenting**: Apply emotional intelligence to better understand and connect with your children, fostering open dialogue and emotional support.

4. **Mentoring and Coaching**: Mentors and coaches can use emotional intelligence to guide and support their mentees effectively.

5. **Community Engagement**: When advocating for social change or participating in community initiatives, emotional intelligence enhances your ability to connect with others and inspire action.

Cultivating Emotional Intelligence in Communication

Mastering emotional intelligence in communication is a lifelong journey of self-awareness and skill development. As you navigate the complexities of interpersonal dynamics, remember that emotional intelligence is the key to connecting on a deeper level and responding to the emotional needs of those you interact with. The knowledge and strategies you gain in this chapter will empower you to communicate more effectively and empathetically. In the following chapters, we'll delve into topics like conflict resolution, inspiring others, and leadership, where emotional intelligence plays a pivotal role. Get ready for more transformative insights and practical guidance.

Chapter 17: Conflict Resolution

Welcome to a chapter that explores the art of conflict resolution. Conflicts are an inevitable part of life, whether in our personal relationships, professional endeavors, or within communities. However, conflicts need not be seen as obstacles but rather as opportunities for growth, understanding, and strengthening connections. In this chapter, we'll delve into the intricacies of conflict resolution, equipping you with the knowledge and strategies to navigate conflicts effectively and transform them into opportunities for positive change.

Understanding Conflict

Before we explore the strategies for effective conflict resolution, let's take a moment to understand the fundamental concepts of conflict.

What Is Conflict?

Conflict is a clash of interests, values, actions, or views between two or more parties. It arises when individuals or groups perceive a threat to their needs, goals, or well-being. Conflicts can manifest in various forms, including disagreements, disputes, or even full-blown confrontations.

The Nature of Conflict

Conflicts can vary in nature:

1. **Interpersonal Conflict**: Arises between individuals due to differences in personality, values, or interests.

2. **Intrapersonal Conflict**: Occurs within an individual, often involving inner dilemmas or struggles.

3. **Inter-group Conflict**: Involves conflicts between two or more groups, such as teams within an organization or different communities.

4. **Inter-cultural Conflict**: Arises due to cultural differences and misunderstandings between individuals from diverse backgrounds.

The Role of Conflict in Personal and Professional Growth

While conflicts are often seen as negative experiences, they can serve as opportunities for growth and self-discovery. Successfully navigating conflicts can lead to:

- Enhanced communication and understanding.

- Improved problem-solving skills.

- Strengthened relationships.

- Personal and professional development.

Strategies for Effective Conflict Resolution

Now, let's explore practical strategies for resolving conflicts and turning them into opportunities for positive change:

Active Listening

Listen Actively

Pay close attention to what the other party is saying and demonstrate understanding.

Avoid Making Assumptions

Avoid making assumptions about the other party's intentions, feelings, or motivations. Seek clarification and gain a clear understanding of their perspective.

Empathy

Practice Empathy

Put yourself in the other party's shoes to comprehend their emotions, needs, and concerns.

Emotion Regulation

During conflicts, practice emotional regulation to keep your emotions in check. Emotional outbursts can escalate conflicts. Instead, express your emotions calmly and constructively.

Effective Communication

Use "I" Statements

For example, say, "I feel frustrated when..." rather than pointing fingers with accusatory language.

Avoid Blame

Blaming others can intensify conflicts. Avoid personal attacks and criticism.

Problem-Solving

Collaborative Problem-Solving

Approach conflicts as problems to be solved collaboratively. Engage in joint problem-solving by seeking solutions that satisfy both parties' needs.

Negotiation

Negotiation involves finding common ground and reaching a compromise that benefits both parties. Seek win-win solutions that address each party's concerns.

Mediation

Mediation by a Neutral Third Party

In situations where conflicts are particularly challenging, consider involving a neutral third party, such as a mediator. Mediators can facilitate communication, guide the process, and help find solutions that everyone can agree on.

Restorative Practices

Restorative practices focus on repairing the harm caused by conflicts and rebuilding trust. This approach is particularly valuable in personal relationships and communities.

Cultural Sensitivity

Cultural Competency

In inter-cultural conflicts, it's essential to be culturally sensitive and competent. Learn about cultural differences and customs to avoid misunderstandings and conflicts based on cultural biases.

Cross-Cultural Mediation

In inter-cultural conflicts, consider cross-cultural mediation, where a mediator with knowledge of both cultures can bridge understanding and facilitate resolution.

Real-Life Examples of Conflict Resolution

To illustrate the power of conflict resolution, let's explore real-life examples where individuals and organizations have successfully navigated conflicts:

1. **Marital Counseling**: Couples who seek counseling often learn effective conflict resolution strategies to strengthen their relationships.

2. **Workplace Mediation**: Many organizations provide mediation services to help employees resolve workplace conflicts, fostering a harmonious work environment.

3. **International Diplomacy**: In international relations, diplomats and negotiators work to resolve conflicts between nations, aiming for peaceful resolutions and diplomacy.

4. **Community Reconciliation**: In communities affected by conflicts or disputes, community leaders and mediators work to restore harmony and understanding.

5. **Business Negotiations**: Skilled negotiators in the business world find mutually beneficial solutions to conflicts, helping companies prosper.

Application of Conflict Resolution in Daily Life

The principles of conflict resolution can be applied in various aspects of daily life:

1. **Personal Relationships**: Enhance your personal connections and resolve conflicts with family and friends by practicing empathy, active listening, and effective communication.

2. **Workplace**: Apply conflict resolution strategies to foster a productive and harmonious work environment by addressing conflicts among colleagues, supervisors, and teams.

3. **Parenting**: Use conflict resolution techniques to guide and support your children in resolving conflicts with peers, siblings, or at school.

4. **Community Engagement**: When participating in community initiatives or advocacy, conflict resolution skills can help you navigate disagreements and promote positive change.

5. **Self-Improvement**: Conflict resolution skills can also be applied to inner conflicts and dilemmas, aiding personal growth and decision-making.

Cultivating Conflict Resolution Skills

Mastering conflict resolution is a lifelong journey of self-awareness and skill development. As you navigate conflicts, remember that they need not be obstacles but opportunities for growth, understanding, and strengthening connections. The knowledge and strategies you gain in this chapter will empower you to navigate conflicts effectively and transform them into opportunities for positive change. In the following chapters, we'll delve into topics like inspiring others, leadership, and effective communication, where conflict resolution skills play a pivotal role. Get ready for more transformative insights and practical guidance.

Chapter 18: The Art of Public Speaking and Presentation

Welcome to a chapter that explores the captivating world of public speaking and presentation. The ability to express your ideas with confidence and clarity in front of an audience is a valuable skill that can open doors to personal, professional, and educational opportunities. In this chapter, we will delve into the art of public speaking and presentation, providing you with the knowledge and strategies to become a more compelling and effective speaker.

The Importance of Public Speaking and Presentation

Before we dive into the strategies for becoming a proficient public speaker, let's understand the significance of this skill in various aspects of life.

Professional Success

Public speaking and presentation skills are often critical for career advancement. Whether you're delivering a pitch to potential clients, presenting to colleagues, or speaking at industry conferences, the ability to convey your ideas persuasively can set you apart in your field.

Educational Advancement

In an educational context, public speaking is essential for students and professionals alike. Whether you're giving class presentations, defending a thesis, or teaching others, strong speaking skills are a key asset.

Personal Growth

Public speaking can boost your self-confidence and self-esteem. It can also enhance your communication skills, making you more adept at conveying your thoughts and ideas in everyday conversations.

The Fundamentals of Public Speaking

To become a proficient public speaker, you need to grasp the fundamentals of this art.

Know Your Audience

Understanding your audience is crucial. Tailor your message, tone, and style to the preferences and expectations of your listeners.

Craft a Clear Message

Your message should be clear and concise. Identify the key points you want to convey and structure your speech or presentation around them.

Practice and Rehearsal

Practice is essential for public speaking. Rehearse your speech or presentation multiple times, refining your delivery, timing, and emphasis. Consider recording yourself for self-assessment.

Overcoming Nervousness

Nervousness is common, even among experienced speakers. To manage your nerves, practice relaxation techniques, such as deep breathing and visualization. Familiarity with your material can also boost your confidence.

Strategies for Effective Public Speaking and Presentation

Now, let's explore practical strategies for becoming a more compelling and effective public speaker.

Engage Your Audience

Start with a Hook

Begin your speech or presentation with a compelling hook. This could be a story, a surprising fact, a rhetorical question, or a quote that piques your audience's interest.

Maintain Eye Contact

Maintaining eye contact with your audience fosters a sense of connection and engagement. Avoid reading your speech verbatim or staring at your notes or slides.

Use Visual Aids Wisely

However, use them sparingly and ensure they complement, rather than overshadow, your message.

Speak Clearly and Slowly

Avoid rushing through your material, as it can make you difficult to understand.

Use Effective Body Language

Your body language communicates a great deal to your audience. Stand confidently, use gestures purposefully, and move with intention to enhance your message.

Master the Art of Storytelling

Use anecdotes and narratives to illustrate your points and create a connection with your listeners.

Encourage Interaction

Where appropriate, engage your audience by asking questions, facilitating discussions, or encouraging participation. Interaction can make your presentation more dynamic and memorable.

Handle Questions and Challenges Gracefully

Be prepared to answer questions and address challenges from your audience. Anticipate potential queries and practice responding calmly and confidently.

Visualize Success

Visualization is a technique that can boost your confidence and reduce anxiety. Before your speech or presentation, visualize yourself delivering it with confidence and receiving a positive response.

Real-Life Examples of Effective Public Speaking

To illustrate the power of effective public speaking, let's explore real-life examples where individuals have used their speaking skills to inspire, inform, and make a lasting impact:

1. **Inspirational Speakers**: Figures like Martin Luther King Jr., Malala Yousafzai, and Nelson Mandela have delivered powerful speeches that spurred change and rallied support for their causes.

2. **Educational Lecturers**: Professors and experts in various fields use their speaking skills to educate and inspire students and peers.

3. **Business Leaders**: Successful entrepreneurs and CEOs often deliver compelling presentations to pitch ideas, secure funding, and motivate their teams.

4. **Politicians**: Politicians use public speaking to gain support, outline policies, and communicate with the public.

5. **Motivational Coaches**: Life coaches and motivational speakers inspire personal growth and transformation through their speeches.

Application of Public Speaking in Daily Life

The principles of public speaking can be applied in various aspects of daily life:

1. **Workplace**: Use your public speaking skills to excel in meetings, pitch ideas, lead presentations, and communicate effectively with colleagues and supervisors.

2. **Education**: Enhance your educational experience by delivering effective presentations, defending your ideas, and teaching others.

3. **Personal Relationships**: Improve your communication with friends and family by speaking confidently and persuasively.

4. **Community Engagement**: Participate in community initiatives, advocacy, or public service by effectively conveying your ideas and motivating others.

5. **Self-Improvement**: Boost your self-confidence and communication skills to further your personal growth and development.

Cultivating Public Speaking Skills

Becoming a proficient public speaker is an ongoing journey of practice and skill development. As you navigate the world of public speaking and presentations, remember that your ability to communicate effectively can open doors to a myriad of opportunities. The knowledge and strategies you gain in this chapter will empower you to become a more compelling and persuasive speaker. In the following chapters, we'll delve into topics like leadership, effective communication, and inspiring others, where your public speaking skills will prove invaluable. Get ready for more transformative insights and practical guidance.

Chapter 19: Networking for Success: Building Meaningful Connections

Welcome to a chapter that explores the art of networking and building meaningful connections. In today's interconnected world, the ability to establish and nurture relationships can be a powerful asset for personal and professional growth. In this chapter, we will delve into the strategies and techniques for successful networking, providing you with the knowledge and skills to build lasting, meaningful connections.

The Power of Networking

Before we dive into the strategies for successful networking, it's essential to understand the significance of networking in various aspects of life.

Professional Success

Networking plays a crucial role in career development. It can lead to job opportunities, mentorship, and valuable insights into your industry.

Personal Growth

Building a network of friends and acquaintances can enhance your personal life by providing support, diverse perspectives, and shared experiences.

Educational Advancement

In an educational context, networking can lead to collaborative projects, research opportunities, and access to resources that can further your academic pursuits.

The Foundations of Effective Networking

To become a proficient networker, you need to establish a strong foundation for your networking efforts.

Authenticity

Be genuine in your interactions. Authenticity is key to building meaningful connections.

Active Listening

Effective networking requires active listening. Pay close attention to what others are saying, ask questions, and show that you genuinely care about their perspectives.

Clarity of Purpose

Have a clear understanding of your networking goals. What do you hope to achieve through your connections? Clarity of purpose guides your networking efforts.

Building Trust

Trust is the bedrock of meaningful connections. Be reliable, keep your commitments, and maintain confidentiality when needed.

Strategies for Successful Networking

Now, let's explore practical strategies for becoming a successful networker and building meaningful connections.

Expand Your Circles

Attend Networking Events

Participate in industry-specific events, conferences, and meetups. These gatherings provide opportunities to connect with like-minded individuals and professionals.

Utilize Social Media

Leverage social media platforms like LinkedIn, Twitter, and Instagram to connect with people in your field or area of interest.

Elevator Pitch

Develop a concise elevator pitch that describes who you are and what you're seeking or offering. An effective elevator pitch makes a strong first impression.

Follow Up

Send a personalized email, connect on social media, or arrange a follow-up meeting. This shows your interest and commitment to building a connection.

Give Before You Receive

Networking is a two-way street. Offer help, share knowledge, or make introductions without expecting an immediate return. Generosity is appreciated and fosters goodwill.

Join Professional Associations

These groups often provide networking opportunities, events, and resources.

Attend Workshops and Seminars

Participate in workshops, seminars, and training sessions. These events can expand your knowledge while connecting you with individuals who share your interests.

Maintain a Network Journal

Keep a journal or digital record of your networking activities. This helps you track your connections, remember details about people, and follow up effectively.

Real-Life Examples of Successful Networking

To illustrate the power of successful networking, let's explore real-life examples where individuals have used their networking skills to advance their careers and personal lives:

1. **Entrepreneurs**: Successful entrepreneurs often credit their network for providing support, mentorship, and even investment opportunities.

2. **Professional Growth**: Individuals seeking career growth have connected with mentors and colleagues who offered guidance and opportunities.

3. **Nonprofit Work**: People working in nonprofit organizations have established connections that led to partnerships, fundraising, and community support.

4. **Authors and Artists**: Writers, artists, and creative professionals have built networks that helped them gain exposure, collaborate with others, and access resources.

5. **Community Engagement**: Those involved in community initiatives and social advocacy have formed networks to raise awareness, mobilize support, and drive change.

Application of Networking in Daily Life

The principles of successful networking can be applied in various aspects of daily life:

1. **Professional Development**: Networking can enhance your career by connecting you with mentors, colleagues, and job opportunities.

2. **Education**: In an educational context, networking can lead to collaborative projects, research opportunities, and valuable insights from peers and professors.

3. **Personal Growth**: Building a network of friends and acquaintances can enhance your personal life by providing support, diverse perspectives, and shared experiences.

4. **Community Engagement**: Networking can be a powerful tool for those involved in community initiatives, advocacy, and social change efforts.

5. **Entrepreneurship**: Entrepreneurs often rely on networking to gain access to resources, mentors, and potential investors.

Cultivating Networking Skills

Becoming a proficient networker is a journey of practice and skill development. As you navigate the world of networking and relationship building, remember that your ability to establish and nurture connections can be a powerful asset. The knowledge and strategies you gain in this chapter will empower you to build lasting, meaningful connections. In the following chapters, we'll delve into topics like leadership, communication, and inspiring others, where your networking skills will prove invaluable. Get ready for more transformative insights and practical guidance.

Chapter 20: Adapting Your Communication to Diverse Audiences

Welcome to a chapter that explores the art of adapting your communication to diverse audiences. In today's multicultural and interconnected world, the ability to tailor your message to different audiences is a valuable skill that can lead to effective communication and stronger relationships. In this chapter, we will delve into the strategies and techniques for adapting your communication to diverse audiences, providing you with the knowledge and skills to connect with a wide range of individuals.

The Importance of Adapting Your Communication

Before we delve into the strategies for adapting your communication to diverse audiences, it's essential to understand the significance of this skill in various aspects of life.

Effective Communication

Adapting your communication to diverse audiences is key to effective communication. It ensures that your message is understood and well-received by a wide range of individuals.

Building Relationships

Understanding the needs and preferences of diverse audiences can help you build stronger and more meaningful relationships with people from various backgrounds.

Conflict Resolution

In situations where conflicts arise, adapting your communication can help de-escalate tensions and find common ground for resolution.

The Foundations of Adapting Your Communication

To become proficient at adapting your communication, you need to establish a strong foundation for your efforts.

Cultural Competency

Cultural competency is essential for understanding the cultural norms, values, and communication styles of different groups. It helps you avoid misunderstandings and promote cross-cultural communication.

Empathy

It plays a crucial role in adapting your communication, as it allows you to connect on a deeper level with diverse audiences.

Active Listening

Active listening is a fundamental skill for adapting your communication. Pay close attention to what others are saying and demonstrate that you understand their perspectives and feelings.

Strategies for Adapting Your Communication to Diverse Audiences

Now, let's explore practical strategies for becoming proficient at adapting your communication to diverse audiences.

Know Your Audience

Research and Prepare

Before communicating with a new audience, conduct research to understand their background, cultural norms, and communication preferences. This preparation will help you tailor your message effectively.

Ask Questions

Ask questions to learn more about your audience's needs, interests, and expectations.

Adjust Your Language

Use Simple and Clear Language

Avoid jargon, complex vocabulary, or idioms that may not be familiar to your audience.

Avoid Slang and Colloquialisms

Slang and colloquial expressions may not be universally understood. Avoid using them, especially when communicating with diverse audiences.

Pay Attention to Non-Verbal Cues

Interpret Non-Verbal Communication

Non-verbal cues, such as body language, facial expressions, and tone of voice, can convey a great deal of information. Pay attention to these cues to understand your audience's feelings and reactions.

Adjust Your Own Non-Verbal Communication

Be mindful of your own non-verbal cues. Ensure that your body language, facial expressions, and tone of voice align with your message and are culturally appropriate.

Use Inclusive Language

Avoid Biased or Offensive Language

Be vigilant about using inclusive language that avoids biases, stereotypes, or offensive terms. Ensure your communication is respectful and considerate of your audience's sensitivities.

Provide Context

Offer Background Information

When discussing complex or unfamiliar topics, provide background information and context to help your audience understand the subject matter.

Clarify Your Message

Ask if your audience has questions or needs clarification. Encourage them to seek additional information to ensure they fully understand your message.

Be Patient

Allow Time for Processing

Recognize that individuals from diverse backgrounds may need more time to process information and respond. Be patient and avoid rushing the communication process.

Encourage Feedback

This open dialogue can enhance mutual understanding and effective communication.

Real-Life Examples of Adapting Your Communication

To illustrate the power of adapting your communication to diverse audiences, let's explore real-life examples where individuals have successfully navigated cross-cultural communication:

1. **International Diplomacy**: Diplomats and negotiators must adapt their communication to diverse audiences when resolving conflicts and building international relationships.

2. **Business and Global Markets**: Companies that operate in global markets must adapt their marketing and communication strategies to connect with diverse customer bases.

3. **Education and Teaching**: Educators who teach diverse student populations adapt their teaching methods and communication to meet the needs of all students.

4. **Healthcare and Patient Communication**: Healthcare providers must adapt their communication to patients from various cultural backgrounds to ensure accurate diagnosis and effective treatment.

5. **Multinational Organizations**: Leaders in multinational organizations adapt their communication to connect with employees, partners, and clients from around the world.

Application of Adapting Your Communication in Daily Life

The principles of adapting your communication to diverse audiences can be applied in various aspects of daily life:

1. **Workplace**: Adapt your communication to colleagues from diverse backgrounds to promote effective collaboration and understanding.

2. **Education**: In educational settings, tailor your communication to students from various cultural backgrounds to create an inclusive learning environment.

3. **Personal Relationships**: Adapt your communication style to connect with friends and family from different cultural backgrounds and with diverse perspectives.

4. **Community Engagement**: When participating in community initiatives, adapt your communication to effectively engage with a diverse group of individuals and promote inclusivity.

5. **Travel and Tourism**: When traveling, adapt your communication to engage with locals and fellow travelers from different cultures.

Cultivating Adaptation Skills

Becoming proficient at adapting your communication to diverse audiences is a journey of practice and skill development. As you navigate the world of diverse communication, remember that your ability to understand, empathize, and connect with individuals from various backgrounds can lead to effective communication and stronger relationships. The knowledge and strategies you gain in this chapter will empower you to adapt your communication successfully.

In the following chapters, we'll delve into topics like leadership, conflict resolution, and inspiring others, where your communication skills will prove invaluable. Get ready for more transformative insights and practical guidance.

In our interconnected world, the ability to adapt your communication to diverse audiences is not only a valuable skill but a vital one. It allows you to break down barriers, foster understanding, and connect with people from various walks of life. Whether you're in the boardroom, the classroom, or your community, the power of communication that transcends differences is immeasurable.

As you continue your journey in this book, you'll find further strategies and practical advice to refine your skills, empower your interactions, and inspire positive change. With every chapter, you're one step closer to becoming a more effective, empathetic, and influential communicator. So, let's embrace the diversity of our world and learn to communicate in ways that resonate with everyone we encounter. Your journey to mastering communication is well underway.

Chapter 21: The Future of Communication: Trends and Technologies

Welcome to a chapter that delves into the exciting realm of the future of communication. In today's fast-paced and ever-evolving digital age, understanding the emerging trends and technologies that shape communication is crucial for staying connected and relevant. In this chapter, we will explore the cutting-edge developments in the field of communication and provide insights into what the future may hold for this essential human endeavor.

The Evolution of Communication

Before we delve into the trends and technologies shaping the future of communication, it's essential to understand the dynamic nature of communication and how it has evolved over time.

Historical Perspective

Communication has come a long way from the days of cave paintings and smoke signals. It has evolved through the invention of the printing press, the telegraph, the telephone, and the internet. Each milestone in communication technology has revolutionized the way we connect with one another.

The Digital Age

The 21st century ushered in the digital age, which has transformed how we communicate. Email, social media, instant messaging, and video calls are now integral to our personal and professional lives.

Emerging Trends in Communication

Let's explore some of the most prominent trends that are shaping the future of communication:

1. Virtual and Augmented Reality (VR/AR)

Virtual and augmented reality are poised to revolutionize communication by immersing users in virtual environments or enhancing the real world with digital information. From virtual meetings to augmented reality applications in education and entertainment, VR and AR offer new dimensions of interaction.

2. Artificial Intelligence (AI)

AI-powered chatbots, virtual assistants, and predictive text are already part of our communication landscape. In the future, AI will play an even more significant role in enhancing the efficiency of communication, automating tasks, and personalizing user experiences.

3. 5G Technology

This will not only improve the quality of video calls but also enable the widespread adoption of Internet of Things (IoT) devices, transforming how we communicate with our surroundings.

4. Blockchain Technology

Blockchain, known for its applications in cryptocurrency, is also being explored for secure and transparent communication, especially in areas like secure messaging and data privacy.

5. Voice and Visual Search

Voice-activated devices and visual search technologies are changing the way we access information. This trend is expected to continue, making voice and visual search a key part of communication.

6. Remote Work and Telecommuting

The COVID-19 pandemic accelerated the shift to remote work and telecommuting. This trend is likely to continue, with more people working from home and collaborating through digital communication tools.

The Role of Technologies in Future Communication

Let's take a closer look at some of the key technologies that will shape the future of communication:

1. 5G Networks

The deployment of 5G networks will bring unprecedented speed and reliability to our internet connections. This will enable high-quality video conferencing, augmented reality experiences, and seamless communication across devices.

2. Artificial Intelligence (AI)

AI will continue to transform how we communicate. AI-powered language translation, chatbots, and predictive text are just the beginning. As AI becomes more sophisticated, it will enhance our communication by providing real-time language translation, personalized content recommendations, and even assistive communication for those with disabilities.

3. Virtual and Augmented Reality (VR/AR)

VR and AR will create immersive communication experiences. Imagine attending virtual meetings, exploring 3D models remotely, or socializing in augmented reality environments. These technologies will redefine how we connect with others.

4. Blockchain

Blockchain technology has the potential to secure communication and data sharing. It can be used to ensure the integrity and privacy of messages, documents, and transactions, making it a powerful tool in the future of communication.

5. Voice and Visual Search

Voice-activated devices like Amazon's Alexa and visual search technologies in platforms like Pinterest are changing the way we access information. As these technologies advance, they will enable more intuitive and efficient communication.

6. Internet of Things (IoT)

From smart homes to wearable devices, the IoT will play a significant role in communication by allowing devices to interact with each other and exchange information, creating a seamless and interconnected world.

The Future of Social Media

Social media platforms have already transformed how we connect and communicate with each other. Here are some potential future developments in social media:

1. Augmented Reality Social Interaction

Social media platforms may integrate augmented reality features that allow users to interact with friends and followers in virtual spaces. This could include shared virtual experiences, virtual concerts, or digital social gatherings.

2. Enhanced Data Privacy

As concerns about data privacy grow, social media platforms are likely to implement more robust privacy features, giving users greater control over their personal data and how it is shared.

3. AI-Personalized Content

Social media algorithms will become even more sophisticated, delivering highly personalized content and recommendations based on users' preferences and behaviors.

4. New Forms of Social Commerce

Social media platforms will continue to evolve as e-commerce hubs. Users will be able to shop directly from their favorite platforms, making the purchasing process more seamless and integrated into the social experience.

5. **Virtual Reality Social Worlds

Virtual reality social worlds will enable users to create and interact with virtual avatars in immersive digital environments. These environments will serve as virtual meeting spaces, event venues, and social hubs, allowing for shared experiences and interactions.

The Future of Business Communication

Communication in the business world is undergoing significant transformation. Here's what the future may hold for business communication:

1. Hybrid Work Models

In the future, many organizations will adopt hybrid work models that combine remote and in-person work, creating new challenges and opportunities for communication.

2. Collaboration Tools

Collaboration tools and project management software will continue to evolve, facilitating efficient communication and collaboration among remote and in-person teams.

3. Data-Driven Decision-Making

Data analytics and business intelligence will play a more prominent role in communication. Organizations will use data to make informed decisions, optimize processes, and enhance communication strategies.

4. AI-Powered Customer Service

AI-powered chatbots and virtual assistants will become even more sophisticated, offering efficient and personalized customer support, improving communication between businesses and their customers.

5. Sustainable Business Practices

Sustainability and corporate social responsibility will impact communication. Businesses will communicate their efforts toward sustainability and engage with environmentally conscious consumers.

Ethical Considerations in Future Communication

As we embrace new communication technologies and strategies, it's crucial to consider the ethical implications of these advancements:

1. Privacy and Data Security

With the growing digital footprint, safeguarding privacy and data security is paramount. Organizations and individuals must prioritize data protection and ensure secure communication.

2. Misinformation and Fake News

The spread of misinformation and fake news is a significant concern in the digital age. Future communication strategies should focus on critical thinking and media literacy to combat this issue.

3. Digital Inclusion

Access to technology and communication tools must be inclusive. Efforts should be made to bridge the digital divide, ensuring that everyone has equal access to the benefits of communication technologies.

4. AI Bias and Fairness

As AI plays a more significant role in communication, it's essential to address issues of bias and fairness in AI algorithms to avoid perpetuating inequalities in communication.

5. Sustainable Communication

The environmental impact of communication technologies should be considered. Sustainable practices should be integrated into the development and use of communication tools.

Preparing for the Future of Communication

In an ever-evolving digital landscape, staying prepared and adaptable is key. Here are some steps to prepare for the future of communication:

1. Continuous Learning

Stay updated on emerging technologies and communication trends through continuous learning and professional development. Courses, webinars, and workshops can help you acquire new skills and knowledge.

2. Adaptability

Cultivate adaptability and openness to change. Embrace new communication tools and strategies, and be willing to adjust your approach as the landscape evolves.

3. Ethical Considerations

Consider the ethical implications of your communication practices. Prioritize privacy, data security, and fairness in your interactions.

4. Sustainability

Consider the environmental impact of your communication tools and practices. Explore ways to reduce your carbon footprint and promote sustainable communication.

5. Collaboration

Embrace collaboration and teamwork. Effective communication in the future will often involve collaborative efforts with colleagues, partners, and even artificial intelligence.

The future of communication is a fascinating and dynamic landscape that promises to transform how we connect, collaborate, and convey our ideas. As technology continues to advance and our world becomes increasingly interconnected, the possibilities for communication are limitless. By staying informed, adaptable, and ethically conscious, you can navigate this ever-evolving landscape with confidence and make the most of the exciting opportunities it offers.

In the chapters that follow, we will continue to explore essential aspects of communication, providing you with the knowledge and skills to thrive in this digital age. Whether you're communicating in your personal life, advancing your career, or driving positive change in your community, the future of communication holds the keys to your success and fulfillment.

Chapter 22: Communication and Leadership: Inspiring Others

Welcome to a chapter that delves into the intersection of communication and leadership. Leadership is not solely about giving orders; it's about inspiring and guiding others to achieve a common goal. In this chapter, we will explore the essential role of communication in inspiring and leading individuals and teams to success.

The Essence of Leadership

Before we dive into the intricacies of communication in leadership, let's understand the essence of leadership itself.

Defining Leadership

Leadership is the art of guiding individuals or groups toward a shared vision, purpose, or objective. A leader is not just someone with authority; they are individuals who can influence and inspire others, whether in a professional, personal, or community context.

Leadership vs. Management

Leadership is often contrasted with management. While management is concerned with tasks, processes, and efficiency, leadership is about people, inspiration, and direction. Effective leaders are not just managers; they are motivators and visionaries.

The Role of Communication in Leadership

Effective leadership depends on clear, persuasive, and empathetic communication. Here's why communication is crucial in leadership:

1. Alignment of Vision

Leaders must convey their vision to their team clearly. Without effective communication, team members may not understand the vision, leading to misalignment and confusion.

2. Inspiration and Motivation

Leaders use communication to inspire and motivate their team. They articulate the "why" behind tasks and projects, making them more meaningful and engaging for team members.

3. Empathy and Understanding

Leaders need to understand their team's needs and concerns. Empathetic communication fosters trust and helps leaders address these needs effectively.

4. Conflict Resolution

Conflicts are inevitable in any group. Leaders must use their communication skills to resolve conflicts and maintain a harmonious work environment.

5. Decision-Making

Leaders often make significant decisions. Effective communication ensures that team members understand the rationale behind these decisions, even if they don't always agree.

Leadership Styles and Communication

Different leadership styles rely on various communication approaches. Let's explore some common leadership styles and how they use communication:

1. Transformational Leadership

Transformational leaders inspire and motivate by creating a compelling vision. Their communication is visionary, passionate, and focused on long-term goals. They encourage innovation and personal growth.

2. Servant Leadership

Their communication is empathetic, focused on listening, and aims to support the personal and professional development of their team.

3. Autocratic Leadership

Their communication tends to be directive and one-way. They provide clear instructions but may not involve others in decision-making.

4. Democratic Leadership

Democratic leaders involve their team in decision-making. They use open and inclusive communication to gather input and make collective decisions.

5. Laissez-Faire Leadership

Laissez-faire leaders give their team autonomy. Their communication is minimal, allowing team members to make their own decisions and solve problems independently.

Effective Communication Strategies for Leaders

To inspire others effectively, leaders must employ specific communication strategies:

1. Active Listening

Active listening is crucial for understanding team members' needs, concerns, and ideas. Leaders should give their full attention, ask clarifying questions, and show empathy.

2. Clarity and Conciseness

Leaders should communicate their vision, expectations, and instructions clearly and concisely.

3. Feedback and Recognition

Leaders should provide regular feedback and recognize team members' contributions. Positive feedback reinforces desired behaviors, while constructive feedback supports growth.

4. Storytelling

Effective leaders often use storytelling to illustrate their vision and values. Stories engage emotions and make messages more memorable.

5. Empathetic Communication

Empathetic communication helps leaders build trust and understanding. Acknowledging team members' feelings and concerns shows that leaders care about their well-being.

Inspiring Teams and Individuals

Inspiring others is a central aspect of leadership. Leaders must know how to motivate both teams and individuals. Here are strategies for doing so:

Motivating Teams

1. **Shared Vision**: Communicate a compelling shared vision that unites the team toward a common goal.

2. **Recognition**: Celebrate team achievements and acknowledge their contributions.

3. **Empowerment**: Encourage team members to take ownership and make decisions collectively.

4. **Challenges**: Present challenges that push the team's capabilities and foster growth.

Motivating Individuals

1. **Personal Growth**: Understand each individual's goals and aspirations and align their role with their personal development.

2. **Clear Expectations**: Communicate clear and achievable expectations for their role.

3. **Feedback**: Provide regular feedback, addressing their strengths and areas for improvement.

4. **Recognition**: Recognize their achievements and celebrate their successes.

Overcoming Leadership Communication Challenges

Leaders may face communication challenges that hinder their ability to inspire others.

1. Resistance to Change

Challenge: Team members may resist change, making it challenging to implement a new vision or strategy.

Strategy: Communicate the reasons for change clearly and emphasize the benefits. Involve team members in the change process, addressing their concerns and encouraging participation.

2. Poor Team Dynamics

Challenge: Team dynamics may be strained due to conflicts or lack of collaboration.

Strategy: Address conflicts promptly, encourage open communication, and create opportunities for team-building activities.

3. Misalignment of Values

Challenge: Team members may have values or goals that are misaligned with the leader's vision.

Strategy: Encourage open discussions about values and find common ground. When values are fundamentally misaligned, consider whether a different role may be a better fit for the team member.

4. Communication Overload

Challenge: Information overload can lead to team members feeling overwhelmed.

Strategy: Prioritize communication and streamline information to focus on what is most essential. Encourage team members to provide input on how information is shared.

5. Lack of Trust

Challenge: A lack of trust can hinder effective communication and collaboration.

Strategy: Build trust through consistent, honest, and transparent communication.

Real-Life Examples of Inspiring Leadership

Let's explore real-life examples of inspiring leadership and how effective communication played a vital role:

1. **Martin Luther King Jr.**: Through his powerful speeches and messages of equality, Martin Luther King Jr. inspired a civil rights movement that changed the course of American history.

2. **Nelson Mandela**: As a leader in the fight against apartheid, Nelson Mandela used his communication skills to unite a divided nation and inspire reconciliation and forgiveness.

3. **Winston Churchill**: During World War II, Winston Churchill's speeches and radio broadcasts rallied the British people and their allies to persevere in the face of adversity.

4. **Oprah Winfrey**: Oprah's ability to connect with her audience through her talk show and other media platforms has inspired

millions and made her a role model for personal development and empowerment.

5. **Elon Musk**: As a visionary entrepreneur, Elon Musk has effectively communicated his bold visions for space exploration, sustainable energy, and technological innovation. His communication style, marked by passion and clear articulation of complex concepts, has garnered support and investment in his ventures.

6. **Malala Yousafzai**: Malala's advocacy for girls' education in the face of adversity showcases the power of her communication skills. Her speeches and writings have inspired a global movement for education and gender equality.

These examples demonstrate that effective communication is not only an essential component of leadership but also a catalyst for transformative change.

Leading Through Challenging Situations

Effective leaders shine through challenging situations, and their communication plays a pivotal role. Here are strategies for leading through adversity:

1. Crisis Communication

In times of crisis, leaders must communicate transparently, providing timely updates and reassurance. Their communication should convey empathy and a clear plan of action.

2. Change Management

Leaders guiding their teams through significant changes should communicate the reasons for change, the expected impact, and the benefits. They should address concerns and involve team members in the transition process.

3. Conflict Resolution

Effective leaders are skilled in resolving conflicts. They use open and empathetic communication to understand the root causes of conflicts and facilitate solutions.

4. Mentoring and Coaching

Leaders should invest in the personal and professional development of their team members. Mentoring and coaching involve communication that provides guidance, feedback, and support.

5. Inspiring Innovation

Leaders should encourage innovative thinking and creative problem-solving. They communicate a culture that values new ideas and the potential for positive change.

The Impact of Leadership Communication

The impact of effective leadership communication extends beyond individual and team success:

Organizational Culture

Leaders set the tone for an organization's culture through their communication. A culture of trust, openness, and collaboration fosters a positive work environment.

Employee Engagement

Engaged employees are more productive and motivated. Leaders who communicate effectively engage their teams and improve overall job satisfaction.

Stakeholder Relations

Leaders often interact with external stakeholders, such as clients, investors, and the public. Their communication can influence the perception of the organization and its reputation.

Personal Growth

Effective leaders not only inspire others but also support their personal and professional growth. The mentorship and guidance they provide through communication contribute to individual development.

Developing Your Leadership Communication Skills

Leadership communication is a skill that can be developed and refined. Here's how you can enhance your leadership communication skills:

1. Self-Awareness

Start by understanding your own communication style, strengths, and areas for improvement. Self-awareness is the foundation for effective leadership communication.

2. Active Listening

Practice active listening to understand your team's needs, concerns, and ideas. Listening is as important as speaking in effective leadership communication.

3. Emotional Intelligence

Develop emotional intelligence to connect with your team on a deeper level. Understand and manage your own emotions while showing empathy for others.

4. Clarity and Conciseness

Work on delivering clear and concise messages. Avoid jargon and ambiguity, ensuring that your team understands your vision and expectations.

5. Feedback and Recognition

Provide regular feedback and recognition. Positive reinforcement and constructive feedback guide your team's growth.

6. Adaptability

Effective leaders can communicate with a wide range of individuals.

7. Conflict Resolution Skills

Learn effective conflict resolution techniques to address disagreements and maintain a harmonious work environment.

8. Mentorship and Coaching

Consider mentoring and coaching team members to support their development. Effective leaders are also mentors and coaches who use communication to guide and empower.

9. Continuous Learning

Stay updated on leadership communication best practices through reading, training, and seeking mentorship from experienced leaders.

Conclusion

Leadership and communication are intertwined, each reinforcing the other. Effective leadership hinges on the ability to communicate a clear vision, inspire and motivate, and foster collaboration and growth. Leaders who invest in their communication skills create engaged and empowered teams and drive positive change within their organizations and communities.

As you continue your leadership journey, remember that leadership communication is not just about words but also about empathy, listening, and actions. By honing your leadership communication skills and embracing diverse leadership styles, you can inspire and guide others to achieve shared goals and make a lasting impact.

Chapter 23: The Art of Persuasion and Negotiation

Welcome to a chapter that explores the intricate and essential skills of persuasion and negotiation. These skills are indispensable in both personal and professional life. Whether you're convincing a colleague, making a sales pitch, or settling a disagreement, mastering the art of persuasion and negotiation will greatly enhance your ability to achieve your desired outcomes and build strong, mutually beneficial relationships.

The Power of Persuasion

Understanding Persuasion

Persuasion is the ability to influence others by presenting compelling arguments, emotional appeals, or evidence to support a particular point of view or action. It's not about manipulation but rather the art of making a convincing case that aligns with the interests of both parties.

The Elements of Persuasion

Successful persuasion often relies on several key elements, including:

1. **Credibility**: Building trust and credibility is crucial.

2. **Appeals to Emotion**: Emotional appeals can be highly persuasive. Understanding the emotional needs and concerns of your audience is essential.

3. **Framing**: How you frame your argument matters. Presenting information in a way that resonates with your audience's values and beliefs increases the likelihood of success.

4. **Social Proof**: People tend to follow the lead of others. Demonstrating that others have found value in your argument or proposal can be persuasive.

5. **Reciprocity**: Offering something of value before asking for something in return can trigger a sense of obligation, making it more likely for the other party to agree.

6. **Consistency**: People tend to be more persuaded by those who are consistent in their beliefs and actions. Highlighting consistency in your argument can make it more persuasive.

The Psychology of Persuasion

Understanding the psychological principles behind persuasion can significantly improve your effectiveness. Concepts like the scarcity principle, the principle of authority, and the principle of commitment and consistency play a role in persuasive communication.

The Art of Negotiation

The Nature of Negotiation

Negotiation is a process of reaching an agreement or settlement through discussion, compromise, and often, give-and-take. Negotiation occurs in various contexts, from business deals to resolving interpersonal conflicts.

The Phases of Negotiation

Negotiation typically involves several phases, including:

1. **Preparation**: Setting your goals, identifying the other party's interests, and gathering information.

2. **Discussion**: Engaging in dialogue with the other party to clarify positions, share information, and explore potential solutions.

3. **Proposals and Counterproposals**: Offering and adjusting proposals based on the information and perspectives shared during the discussion phase.

4. **Agreement**: Reaching a mutually acceptable agreement and documenting the terms.

5. **Implementation**: Carrying out the terms of the agreement.

6. **Review and Feedback**: Reflecting on the negotiation process and the outcomes achieved.

The Art of Effective Negotiation

Effective negotiation requires a set of skills and strategies, including:

1. **Active Listening**: Paying close attention to the other party's perspectives and concerns.

2. **Communication**: Clearly and assertively articulating your own interests and needs.

3. **Emotional Intelligence**: Understanding and managing your own emotions and empathizing with the emotions of the other party.

4. **Problem-Solving**: Approaching negotiation as a joint problem-solving endeavor, seeking solutions that benefit both parties.

5. **Flexibility**: Being open to alternative solutions and compromises.

6. **Patience**: Recognizing that negotiation often takes time and multiple interactions.

7. **Ethics**: Maintaining a commitment to ethical conduct and fairness throughout the negotiation process.

The Synergy of Persuasion and Negotiation

The Role of Persuasion in Negotiation

Persuasion is an integral part of negotiation. Whether you're proposing a solution, justifying your position, or trying to build rapport, persuasive communication enhances your ability to influence the other party.

The Role of Negotiation in Persuasion

Negotiation provides a structured framework for persuading others to reach an agreement. It allows you to apply persuasive tactics within a defined context, making it more likely to achieve your desired outcome.

Real-Life Applications

Business Negotiations

Business negotiations are a common and impactful context for applying persuasion and negotiation skills. Whether you're closing a deal, setting the terms of a partnership, or negotiating a contract, the ability to persuade and negotiate effectively can significantly impact your bottom line.

Conflict Resolution

In personal and professional relationships, conflicts are inevitable. Persuasion and negotiation skills are invaluable in resolving disputes, finding common ground, and maintaining healthy relationships.

Sales and Marketing

Sales and marketing professionals rely heavily on persuasion to influence buying decisions. Negotiation also plays a role in closing deals and agreements with clients and partners.

Advocacy and Activism

Advocates and activists use persuasion to build support for their causes and to rally people to take action. Negotiation can come into play when seeking compromises or agreements with authorities or opposing parties.

Diplomacy

In international relations, diplomacy involves complex negotiations and persuasive communication to address global issues, build alliances, and prevent conflicts.

The Ethics of Persuasion and Negotiation

Ethical considerations are paramount when using persuasion and negotiation skills. It's essential to ensure that the techniques employed are fair, transparent, and respectful of the other party's rights and interests. Unethical persuasion or negotiation can damage relationships and reputation.

Practical Strategies for Persuasion and Negotiation

Establishing Common Ground

Start by finding common ground with the other party. Identify shared interests or goals that can serve as a foundation for negotiation. This common ground creates a sense of collaboration and helps build rapport.

Active Listening

Effective listening is a cornerstone of both persuasion and negotiation. By actively listening to the other party's concerns and perspectives, you gain valuable insights that can inform your approach.

Framing Your Argument

Present your case in a way that aligns with the values and priorities of the other party. Framing your argument to resonate with their perspective can make it more persuasive.

Building Trust

Trust is essential in persuasion and negotiation. Demonstrating integrity, reliability, and consistency in your communication builds trust over time.

Balancing Assertiveness and Cooperation

Negotiation often requires a balance between assertiveness and cooperation. While you need to assert your interests, being cooperative and open to compromise can lead to more favorable outcomes.

Emotional Intelligence

Understanding and managing your own emotions and empathizing with the emotions of the other party is vital. Emotional intelligence can help you navigate emotionally charged situations and build rapport.

Overcoming Challenges

Resistance

In some cases, the other party may resist persuasion and negotiation. Overcoming resistance may require patience, relationship-building, and a deep understanding of their concerns and objections.

Deadlocks

Negotiations can reach deadlocks where neither party is willing to budge. To overcome deadlocks, creative problem-solving, compromise, or revisiting the negotiation's objectives may be necessary.

Ethical Dilemmas

Ethical dilemmas can arise when persuasion and negotiation are employed. It's essential to maintain ethical conduct and prioritize fairness, even when facing challenging decisions.

Cultural Differences

In international negotiations or diverse environments, cultural differences can impact communication and negotiation. Sensitivity to cultural nuances is essential to navigate these differences effectively and build trust.

Power Imbalances

Negotiations may involve power imbalances, such as when dealing with a more influential party. In such situations, skillful persuasion and negotiation become even more critical to level the playing field and achieve fair outcomes.

Lack of Information

In some negotiations, you may lack complete information about the other party's interests or options. Overcoming this challenge may involve conducting research or engaging in open dialogue to uncover hidden information.

Real-Life Success Stories

Let's explore real-life examples of successful persuasion and negotiation:

1. **Nelson Mandela**: Mandela's ability to negotiate and persuade was instrumental in ending apartheid in South Africa. His negotiation skills led to a peaceful transition of power and reconciliation.

2. **Martin Luther King Jr.**: Through persuasive speeches and peaceful protests, King successfully advocated for civil rights and racial equality in the United States.

3. **The Camp David Accords**: In 1978, U.S. President Jimmy Carter, Egyptian President Anwar Sadat, and Israeli Prime Minister Menachem Begin negotiated the Camp David Accords, a historic peace agreement between Egypt and Israel.

4. **Elon Musk's SpaceX Contracts**: Elon Musk's SpaceX has secured contracts with NASA and commercial clients through persuasive proposals and negotiations.

5. **Labor Union Negotiations**: Labor unions negotiate with employers to secure better working conditions, benefits, and fair wages for their members. Successful negotiation leads to improved working conditions for employees.

6. **Sales and Marketing Campaigns**: Effective marketing and sales campaigns employ persuasion techniques to influence consumer decisions and close deals.

Applying Persuasion and Negotiation in Daily Life

These skills are not limited to specific contexts; they can be applied in your daily life to:

- Resolve conflicts within your family or with friends.

- Influence decisions within community organizations or volunteer groups.

- Negotiate terms with contractors, service providers, or suppliers.

- Persuade your employer for a raise or promotion.

- Navigate interpersonal disagreements and misunderstandings.

Building Your Persuasion and Negotiation Skills

The ability to persuade and negotiate effectively is a continuous learning process. Consider these strategies to develop and refine these skills:

1. **Education**: Seek books, courses, and resources on persuasion and negotiation to gain insights and techniques.

2. **Practice**: Engage in role-playing scenarios to practice and refine your skills in a safe environment.

3. **Observation**: Learn from effective persuaders and negotiators in your life and industry. Observe their techniques and approaches.

4. **Feedback**: Seek feedback from mentors or trusted colleagues to identify areas for improvement.

5. **Self-awareness**: Reflect on your own communication style and emotional responses to enhance your self-awareness.

6. **Networking**: Connect with professionals who excel in persuasion and negotiation to learn from their experiences.

7. **Mentorship**: Consider finding a mentor who can provide guidance and insights based on their expertise.

Conclusion

Persuasion and negotiation are not just skills for the business world; they are life skills that can enhance your ability to influence decisions, build relationships, and resolve conflicts. Mastering the art of persuasion and negotiation requires a deep understanding of human psychology, effective communication, and ethical conduct.

As you continue your journey to master these skills, remember that they are not about manipulation but about creating mutually beneficial outcomes and fostering understanding. Whether you're advocating for a cause, closing a business deal, or resolving a personal conflict, the art of persuasion and negotiation will empower you to navigate life's complex and diverse challenges with confidence and success.

Chapter 24: Storytelling as a Communication Tool

Welcome to a chapter that delves into the remarkable world of storytelling and its profound impact on communication. Throughout human history, storytelling has been a powerful means of connecting, teaching, and inspiring. In this chapter, we will explore the art of storytelling, its significance in communication, and how you can harness its potential to captivate your audience, convey your messages, and leave a lasting impression.

The Essence of Storytelling

Understanding Storytelling

Storytelling is the art of conveying information, emotions, or experiences through the use of narrative. A well-crafted story has the ability to engage, inform, entertain, and influence an audience. It weaves together characters, events, and emotions to create a compelling and memorable narrative.

The Elements of a Story

1. **Characters**: Relatable figures who drive the narrative and connect with the audience.

2. **Setting**: The backdrop against which the story unfolds, providing context and atmosphere.

3. **Plot**: The sequence of events that drives the story's progression.

4. **Conflict**: A central challenge or problem that characters must address.

5. **Resolution**: The culmination of the story, where conflicts are resolved, and lessons are learned.

6. **Theme**: The central message or moral of the story.

163

The Power of Storytelling

Why Stories Matter

Stories are an integral part of human communication and culture for several reasons:

1. **Engagement**: Stories captivate and maintain the audience's attention, making them more receptive to the message.

2. **Relatability**: Characters and situations in stories often resonate with the audience's own experiences, fostering empathy and understanding.

3. **Memorability**: People remember stories far more effectively than dry facts or statistics.

4. **Emotional Impact**: Stories can evoke a wide range of emotions, allowing for a deeper connection with the audience.

5. **Persuasion**: Stories have the power to persuade by illustrating a point or moral in a relatable context.

6. **Universal Appeal**: Stories transcend cultural and language barriers, making them accessible to diverse audiences.

The Science of Storytelling

Cognitive science and psychology have shown that stories activate various regions of the brain, enhancing both comprehension and retention. This makes storytelling a valuable tool for effective communication.

Storytelling in Different Contexts

Business and Marketing

In the business world, storytelling is a vital tool for branding, marketing, and conveying the mission and values of a company.

Compelling narratives can attract customers, build trust, and differentiate a brand in a competitive market.

Education

Teachers use storytelling to engage students, simplify complex concepts, and create memorable learning experiences. Stories make learning enjoyable and relatable.

Advocacy and Social Change

Advocates and activists use storytelling to raise awareness, build empathy, and mobilize support for various causes. Personal stories can be powerful tools for social change.

Leadership

Leaders often use storytelling to inspire and guide their teams. A well-timed and relevant story can motivate individuals and communicate a vision effectively.

Personal Development

In personal growth and self-help literature, stories serve as examples and metaphors for life lessons. They help readers connect with and apply principles for personal improvement.

The Art of Effective Storytelling

Crafting a Compelling Narrative

Creating a compelling story involves several key steps:

1. **Start with a Hook**: Begin with an attention-grabbing opening that piques the audience's curiosity.

2. **Develop Engaging Characters**: Create relatable characters that the audience can connect with emotionally.

3. **Establish a Setting**: Describe the environment and context where the story takes place.

4. **Build Tension**: Introduce a conflict or challenge that drives the plot forward.

5. **Use Descriptive Language**: Paint vivid images with words to immerse the audience in the story.

6. **Create a Resolution**: Conclude the story by resolving the conflict or leaving the audience with a meaningful message.

Connecting with Emotion

Emotion is a potent tool in storytelling. The audience should feel a connection to the characters and become emotionally invested in the story. This emotional engagement enhances the impact of the narrative.

Relatability and Universality

While stories should be relatable to the audience, they can also contain universal themes and messages that resonate with a broader range of people.

Consistency and Authenticity

Consistency in storytelling ensures that the narrative flows smoothly, while authenticity builds trust with the audience. Authentic stories are more compelling and believable.

Applying Storytelling Techniques

Presentation Skills

In public speaking or presentations, storytelling can make complex information more accessible and engaging. Stories help illustrate key points and maintain the audience's interest.

Marketing and Branding

Companies often use storytelling in their marketing and branding efforts to connect with customers on a personal level. Compelling brand stories can shape consumer perceptions and loyalty.

Conflict Resolution

Storytelling can be a powerful tool in conflict resolution by allowing each party to share their perspective and emotions. This can foster understanding and empathy, leading to resolution.

Teaching and Training

Educators and trainers use storytelling to convey lessons and information in an engaging and memorable way. Stories make learning more enjoyable and effective.

Personal Development

In self-help and personal development literature, stories provide relatable examples of challenges and triumphs. These stories inspire and guide individuals in their personal growth journey.

The Ethics of Storytelling

Ethical considerations are important when using storytelling. It's crucial to be truthful and transparent, avoiding manipulation or exploitation. Stories should serve to enlighten and empower, not deceive or harm.

Practical Strategies for Effective Storytelling

Here are some practical strategies for becoming a better storyteller:

1. **Know Your Audience**: Tailor your story to the interests and needs of your audience.

2. **Practice**: Hone your storytelling skills through practice and feedback.

3. **Use Emotion**: Infuse your story with emotions to connect with your audience.

4. **Create Vivid Imagery**: Use descriptive language to help the audience visualize the story.

5. **Keep it Concise**: Be mindful of the story's length, ensuring it doesn't become overly long or lose the audience's interest.

6. **Have a Clear Message**: Every story should convey a clear message or lesson.

7. **Seek Inspiration**: Draw inspiration from books, movies, real-life experiences, and other storytellers.

Storytelling is an art, a science, and a powerful communication tool. Whether you're a business professional, educator, advocate, leader, or simply someone seeking to engage and connect with others, the ability to tell compelling stories is a skill that can transform your communication. As you continue your journey of exploration and improvement in storytelling, remember that each story has the potential to enlighten, entertain, and inspire, making the world a more connected and compassionate place.

Chapter 25: Crisis Communication: Managing Challenges Effectively

In this chapter, we will dive into the critical realm of crisis communication. Whether you're a business leader, a public figure, or an individual navigating life's unexpected challenges, the ability to manage crises effectively through communication is a valuable skill. This chapter explores the principles, strategies, and practical techniques of crisis communication to help you respond to adversity with poise, transparency, and resilience.

The Nature of Crises

Understanding Crises

A crisis is an unexpected and often challenging event that threatens the normal operation of an organization or an individual's well-being. Crises can take various forms, including natural disasters, financial downturns, public relations crises, health emergencies, and personal setbacks.

The Impact of Crises

The consequences of crises may include financial losses, reputational damage, emotional distress, and physical harm. Effective crisis communication is essential to mitigate these consequences.

The Role of Communication in Crisis Management

Why Communication Matters

Communication is a cornerstone of crisis management for several reasons:

1. **Transparency**: Transparent communication fosters trust and credibility during challenging times.

2. **Information Dissemination**: Communication is the primary means of disseminating essential information to affected parties.

3. **Reputation Management**: Managing the narrative through communication can minimize reputational damage.

4. **Stakeholder Engagement**: Effective communication engages stakeholders and demonstrates care and empathy.

5. **Crisis Resolution**: Communication plays a crucial role in resolving the crisis and guiding recovery efforts.

The Communication Challenge

Crisis communication presents unique challenges, including managing uncertainty, addressing a broad range of emotions, and making decisions under pressure. Adapting to these challenges is essential for effective crisis communication.

Principles of Effective Crisis Communication

Honesty and Transparency

Honesty and transparency are foundational principles in crisis communication. Concealing information or providing misleading information can erode trust and escalate the crisis. Open and honest communication is essential.

Empathy and Compassion

Expressing empathy and compassion for those affected by the crisis demonstrates care and support. Understanding and addressing the emotional impact of the crisis is crucial.

Timeliness

Timely communication is vital during a crisis. Delays in providing information can lead to confusion and speculation. Immediate, relevant updates help to manage the situation effectively.

170

Consistency

Consistency in messaging ensures that information remains accurate and aligned. Consistent communication builds confidence and minimizes confusion.

Accessibility

Information should be accessible to all stakeholders, including those with disabilities or language barriers. Accessibility ensures that everyone can receive critical updates.

Agility

Crisis situations are dynamic and can change rapidly. Being agile in adapting communication strategies and messages to evolving circumstances is crucial.

Preparedness

Preparedness involves having a crisis communication plan in place before a crisis occurs. This plan includes key contacts, messaging templates, and a designated spokesperson.

Crisis Communication Strategies

Identify Key Messages

Identify the core messages you want to convey during the crisis. These messages should address the nature of the crisis, actions being taken, and expectations for stakeholders.

Select Communication Channels

Choose the appropriate communication channels for reaching your target audience. This may include social media, press releases, email, or in-person briefings.

Designate a Spokesperson

Select a trusted and skilled spokesperson to deliver key messages. This person should be well-prepared and capable of handling media inquiries.

Monitor and Respond

Stay vigilant in monitoring the situation and the public response.

Address Rumors and Misinformation

Rumors and misinformation can spread rapidly during a crisis. Address them with accurate information and corrections.

Empower Employees

Empower your internal team to communicate effectively. Ensure they have the information and resources they need to respond to inquiries from colleagues and clients.

The Challenges of Crisis Communication

Managing Stakeholder Emotions

Stakeholders may experience a range of emotions during a crisis, including fear, anger, and confusion. Effective communication should acknowledge and address these emotions.

Balancing Transparency with Legal and Ethical Constraints

While transparency is crucial, legal and ethical considerations may limit the information that can be shared. Striking the right balance is challenging.

Navigating Media and Public Scrutiny

Media and public attention can intensify during a crisis. Managing media inquiries and public scrutiny requires a strategic approach.

Case Studies: Crisis Communication in Action

This section explores real-life examples of crisis communication, including successes and challenges faced by organizations and public figures.

Crisis Communication in Personal Life

Crisis communication is not limited to organizations. Individuals can also benefit from effective communication when facing personal crises, such as health issues, financial setbacks, or family emergencies.

Ethics in Crisis Communication

Ethical considerations are paramount in crisis communication. Upholding honesty, transparency, and compassion while respecting privacy and legal constraints is essential.

Crisis Communication in the Digital Age

The rise of social media and online platforms has transformed crisis communication. This section delves into the unique challenges and opportunities presented by the digital age.

Preparing for the Next Crisis

Effective crisis communication requires preparation. This chapter outlines steps to develop a crisis communication plan and build the necessary skills to navigate future challenges.

Conclusion

Crisis communication is a vital skill for individuals and organizations alike. When confronted with adversity, effective communication can make the difference between chaos and control, between reputational damage and resilience. As you continue to explore the principles, strategies, and ethical considerations of crisis communication, remember that it is a skill that can be cultivated and refined, ultimately helping you navigate crises with grace, empathy, and strength.

Conclusion

Congratulations on embarking on your journey to communication mastery. Throughout this book, you've explored the diverse landscape of effective communication, from understanding the fundamental principles to applying practical techniques in various contexts. As you reach the end of this transformative journey, let's recap some key takeaways and emphasize the importance of committing to ongoing improvement.

Recap of Key Takeaways

The Power of Communication

You've learned that communication is the foundation of human connection. It influences your personal and professional relationships, shapes your impact on others, and is integral to success in various aspects of life.

Effective Communication

Effective communication involves clarity, empathy, active listening, and adaptability. By mastering these elements, you can convey your message more efficiently and connect with your audience on a deeper level.

Context Matters

You've discovered that effective communication is context-dependent. Tailoring your communication style to the situation and audience is essential. Whether it's public speaking, negotiation, or interpersonal relationships, understanding the context is key to success.

Active Listening

Active listening is the cornerstone of effective communication. It involves not only hearing words but also understanding emotions, intentions, and unspoken messages. Practicing active listening enhances your ability to connect and respond thoughtfully.

Non-Verbal Communication

You've learned to recognize and utilize non-verbal communication to enhance your effectiveness in both personal and professional interactions.

Overcoming Obstacles

Communication obstacles, such as misunderstandings, conflicts, and cultural differences, are inevitable. You've explored strategies to navigate these challenges, fostering better communication and stronger relationships.

Persuasion and Influence

The art of persuasion and negotiation is a valuable skill for achieving personal and professional goals. You've uncovered the principles and techniques to persuade, negotiate, and navigate complex discussions.

Storytelling

Storytelling is a powerful communication tool. You've gained insight into crafting compelling narratives that engage, inform, and inspire. Stories are a vehicle for connecting with others on a deeper level.

Crisis Communication

Crises can strike unexpectedly. You've learned the principles and strategies of effective crisis communication, emphasizing transparency, empathy, and preparedness. Crisis communication is a skill that can mitigate the impact of adversity.

Ongoing Growth

Commit to ongoing improvement by practicing, seeking feedback, and adapting your communication skills to evolving contexts and challenges.

Committing to Ongoing Improvement

As you conclude this journey to communication mastery, remember that the learning process is never-ending. The skills and principles you've acquired in this book are the foundation upon which you can build. Here are some steps to commit to ongoing improvement:

1. **Practice Regularly**: Continue to apply the techniques you've learned in real-life situations.

2. **Seek Feedback**: Invite feedback from peers, mentors, or communication experts to identify areas for improvement. Constructive feedback is invaluable.

3. **Adapt to Change**: The world of communication is dynamic, influenced by evolving technologies and cultural shifts. Stay open to adapting your communication style to new contexts.

4. **Empathy and Compassion**: Cultivate empathy and compassion in your interactions. These qualities are essential for understanding others and building meaningful relationships.

5. **Ethical Communication**: Uphold ethical communication in all situations.

6. **Lifelong Learning**: Continue to explore resources, books, courses, and experiences that contribute to your communication mastery.

7. **Mentorship**: Consider mentorship or coaching to receive guidance and insights from experienced communicators.

Your journey to communication mastery is a continual process of growth, refinement, and adaptation. By dedicating yourself to ongoing improvement, you empower yourself to connect more deeply, influence more effectively, and navigate life's challenges with resilience. Communication is not just a skill; it's a tool that can enrich every facet of your life.

A Gift for Your Personal Development

As a token of appreciation for your commitment to personal development and your journey to communication mastery, we are delighted to offer you this valuable bonus: "Mindfulness-Based Stress and Anxiety Management Tools."

This bonus e-book is designed to provide you with practical tools and techniques to help you manage and alleviate these challenges through mindfulness.

What to Expect

In this e-book, you will discover:

- **Understanding Stress and Anxiety**: Gain insights into the nature of stress and anxiety, and how they impact your well-being.

- **Introduction to Mindfulness**: Explore the fundamentals of mindfulness and its role in managing stress and anxiety.

- **Mindful Breathing and Meditation**: Learn mindfulness exercises and meditation practices that promote relaxation and calm.

- **Stress Reduction Techniques**: Discover a variety of techniques to reduce stress and anxiety, such as progressive muscle relaxation and deep breathing.

- **Mindful Living**: Embrace mindfulness as a way of life and learn how to incorporate it into your daily routines.

- **Practical Tips and Exercises**: Access practical exercises and tips that you can apply in your daily life to cultivate mindfulness and reduce stress.

Your Path to Well-Being

We understand that your journey to communication mastery is not just about enhancing your professional and personal interactions; it's also about nurturing your overall well-being. Stress and anxiety can be significant barriers to effective communication, personal growth, and success. By integrating mindfulness-based tools into your life, you can enhance your resilience, emotional intelligence, and overall quality of life.

How to Access Your Bonus

To access "Mindfulness-Based Stress and Anxiety Management Tools," simply click the link provided below, and you can start benefiting from this valuable resource immediately. It's our gift to you as a token of our appreciation for your commitment to personal development and communication mastery.

Download Your Bonus E-Book Here

We hope you find this bonus e-book to be a valuable companion on your journey to enhanced well-being and effective communication. Thank you for being a part of our community, and we look forward to continuing to support your growth and development.

About the Author

Richard Davids is a seasoned communication expert dedicated to helping individuals unlock their communication potential. With a passion for empowering others to connect effectively, Richard has spent years honing his skills in various communication contexts, from public speaking to interpersonal relationships.

As an accomplished author, Richard's work focuses on practical communication strategies that enhance personal and professional lives. His commitment to personal development and his belief in the transformative power of effective communication are at the core of his writing.

Richard Davids is not only a writer but a communicator, mentor, and advocate for the art of meaningful dialogue. His mission is to inspire and guide others on their journey to communication mastery, fostering understanding, connection, and personal growth.

www.ingramcontent.com/pod-product-compliance
Lightning Source LLC
Chambersburg PA
CBHW070008300526
45794CB00001B/240